Living LANGUAGE

ORIGINAL WRITING

Peter Simpson

Hodder & Stoughton

A MEMBER OF THE HODDER HEADLINE GROUP

Acknowledgements

Thanks to past students Nigel, Rachel, Adam Pow, Dan Simpson and Alexandra Hopkins for permission to use material they submitted as coursework during their A-Level course.

To N. J. Warburton (Nick) for permission to use the extract from *The Messenger*.

To Audrey Jones, Alan Butt and Michelle Alcock for permission to reproduce the board game *Knock Out*.

Every effort has been made to trace copyright holders of material reproduced in this book. Any rights not acknowledged will be acknowledged in subsequent printings if notice is given to the publisher.

Orders: please contact Bookpoint Ltd, 130 Milton Park, Abingdon, Oxon OX14 4SB. Telephone: (44) 01235 400414, Fax: (44) 01235 400454. Lines are open from 9.00–6.00, Monday to Saturday, with a 24 hour message answering service. Email address: orders@bookpoint.co.uk

British Library Cataloguing in Publication Data
A catalogue entry for this title is available from The British Library

ISBN 0 340 73080 3

First published 1999
Impression number   10 9 8 7 6 5 4
Year   2005 2004 2003 2002 2001

Cover photo from The Ronald Grant Archive

Typeset by Fakenham Photosetting Ltd, Fakenham, Norfolk NR21 8NL
Printed in Great Britain for Hodder & Stoughton Educational, a division of Hodder Headline Plc, 338 Euston Road, London NW1 3BH by
J. W. Arrowsmith Ltd., Bristol.

Contents

Introduction

As you are reading this the likelihood is that you are studying either an English Language A-Level course or a combined Language and Literature course. It is also likely that you have to produce one or more pieces of writing of your own, either as coursework or under examination conditions.

This volume aims to help you create a range of writing by showing examples of different styles, genre and writing purposes and suggesting ways of developing your own skills as a writer.

There will also be suggestions on the construction of commentaries on your own work: what to include and what to leave out, how to achieve a balance between narrative and analysis, how to match language and format to your target audience and a consideration of the pre-commentary.

There will also be examples of work produced by students either as coursework or under examination conditions.

The terminology may differ from syllabus to syllabus, for example, Original Writing or Language Production, as may the number of pieces required and the total word count but there are features common to all syllabuses. These include a consideration of the audience for the piece of writing, the aims of the writer in terms of its purpose, where the piece might appear and an evaluation of the writing process and the success or otherwise of the piece.

If you have followed a GCSE English course you will have written for different purposes using different formats already. The chances are, however, that you were directed in what you wrote. Your A-Level English course should be a chance to write what you want to. No doubt there will be times when you are instructed by your teacher to produce a certain type of writing. Class writing is a very useful exercise, but for your coursework submission or what you write under examination conditions (if this is a requirement of your particular syllabus) you are the author and what you write is your responsibility.

1 Parody, Pastiche and Satire

This book opens with these topics because they are very popular with students and also because parody, pastiche and satire make a writer look very closely at language choices and audience, factors which are important to all of the purposes of original writing, and in the writing of commentaries.

You will probably be familiar with the techniques of writing on a subject in a style not usually associated with that subject. An example of this would be to take a nursery rhyme or fairy tale and using the basic structure of the original, treat it in a very different way. For example, *Humpty Dumpty* as a police report into a suspected suicide, or *Hansel and Gretel* as a social worker's report into child care. Strictly speaking this is parodic writing. Though the style is totally different to the original, there are enough elements remaining in the new text for the model to be recognised. Parody can also be a mocking imitation of a writer's style exaggerating features of the original by using parallels of form and style.

Pastiches are related to parody in that the writer of a pastiche relies on borrowings from other works but the pastiche can be written in admiration and is not necessarily an attempt to mock.

Satire is an attack, verbally or in writing, which is meant to ridicule a person, an object or another text. One of the best definitions for 'satire' is the description of the Chinese character (the system of pictograms used in Chinese writing) for it – 'laughter with knives'. Satire can be linked to both parody and pastiche but is not an essential element in either.

Parody

In October 1952 the American magazine *Mad* began publication. Its stock in trade was parody. Its writers and artists took many aspects of American popular culture for their inspiration. Comic books, television shows and films were particular targets for the creators of *Mad*. In quick succession appeared *Superduperman, Bat Boy and Rubin* and *Woman Wonder*, based on super hero comics. *Melvin of the Apes* and *Flesh Garden* owed their cartoon existence to the filmed versions of *Tarzan* and *Flash Gordon* while *Dragged Net* was based on the popular detective series *Dragnet*. Shakespeare's *Julius Caesar* (Text 1) not only gave rise to a comic strip parody of the 1953 film

produced by Joseph L. Mankiewicz but also a 'hip' version of Marc
Antony's funeral oration over the body of Caesar (Text 2). We shall return
to the original Shakespearean script when considering the language of
persuasion on p 28.

TEXT 1

Antony:

> Friends, Romans, countrymen, lend me your ears;
> I come to bury Caesar, not to praise him.
> The evil that men do lives after them;
> The good is oft interred with their bones;
> So let it be with Caesar. The noble Brutus
> Hath told you Caesar was ambitious:
> If it were so, it was a grievous fault,
> And grievously hath Caesar answer'd it.
> Here, under leave of Brutus and the rest –
> For Brutus is an honourable man;
> So are they all, all honourable men –
> Come I to speak in Caesar's funeral.
> He was my friend, faithful and just to me:
> But Brutus says he was ambitious;
> And Brutus is an honourable man.
> He hath brought many captives home to Rome
> Whose ransoms did the general coffers fill:
> Did this in Caesar seem ambitious?
> When that the poor have cried, Caesar hath wept:
> Ambition should be made of sterner stuff:
> Yet Brutus says he was ambitious;
> And Brutus is an honourable man.
> You all did see that on the Lupercal
> I thrice presented him a kingly crown,
> Which he did thrice refuse: was this ambition?
> Yet Brutus says he was ambitious;
> And sure he is an honourable man.
> I speak not to disprove what Brutus spoke,
> But I am here to speak what I do know.
> You all did love him once, not without cause:
> What cause withholds you then, to mourn for him?
> O judgement! thou art fled to brutish beasts,
> And men have lost their reason. Bear with me;
> My heart is in the coffin there with Caesar,
> And I must pause till it come back to me.

Julius Caesar by William Shakespeare Act 3, Scene 2 (Lines 75–109)

TEXT 2

The Ides of Mad
Friends, Romans, Hipsters,
Let me clue you in;
I come to put down Caesar, not to groove him.
The square kicks that some cats are on stay with them;
The hip bits, like, go down under;
So let it lay with Caesar. The cool Brutus
Gave you the message Caesar had big eyes;
If that's the sound, someone's copping a plea,
And, like, old Caesar really set them straight.
Here, copacetic* with Brutus and the studs, –
For Brutus is a real cool cat;

So are they all, all cool cats, –
Come I to make this gig at Caesar's lay me;
He was my boy, the most and real gone to me;
But, like, Brutus pegs him as having big eyes;
And Brutus is a real cool cat.
He copped a lot of swinging heads for home,
Which put us way out with that loot;
Does this give Caesar big eyes?
When the square cats bawled, Caesar flipped;
Big eyes should be made of more solid 'megillah';
Yet Brutus pegs him as having big eyes:
And Brutus is a real cool cat.
You all dug that scene at the Lupercal scene
Three times I bugged him with the king's lid,
And three times he hung me up; was this big eyes?
Yet Brutus pegs him with big eyes;
And, sure, he is real cool cat.
I don't want to double-O what Brutus gummed,
But, like, I only dig what comes on straight.
You all got a charge out of him once,
So how come you don't cry the blues for him?
Man! You are real nowhere,
You don't make it anymore. Don't cut out on me;
My guts are in the pad there with Caesar,
And I gotta stop swinging till they round trip.

*US. slang meaning 'excellent' – origin obscure

COMMENTARY The writer of *The Ides of Mad* has drawn on a core lexis of beat slang, the language of jazz fans and beatniks, the key words being: hip/hipster, cool, square, cat(s), pegs, flipped, dug, bugged, lid and cut out, some of which are listed in *Webster's New Collegiate Dictionary* which offers the following explanations:

- Hip – variant of 'hep' – characterised by a keen informed awareness in the newest developments – origin obscure.
- Cool – marked by restrained emotion, excellent.
- Square – a person who is overly conventional or conservative.
- Cat – a player or devotee of hot jazz.
- Dig – to pay attention to, appreciate.
- Flipped – to react violently.

Shakespeare's foregrounded phrases, *Caesar was ambitious* and *Brutus is an honourable man*, are echoed in the parody by *Caesar had big eyes* and *Brutus is a real cool cat*.

It is also of interest that while 'cool' is almost standard English today other slang terms have dropped out of use. 'Lid' is not often used to mean hat now and 'bugged' would possibly be taken to mean something to do with electronic listening devices.

ACTIVITY 1

Read this short extract from the 'To be, or not to be' speech from *Hamlet* carefully and rewrite it in your own slang. For example, would a character from *Eastenders* begin, 'To top meself, or not to top meself, that's the issue here.'?

TEXT 3

To be, or nor to be, that is the question:
Whether 'tis nobler in the mind to suffer
The slings and arrows of outrageous fortune,
Or to take up arms against a sea of troubles
And by opposing end them. To die: to sleep;
No more; and by a sleep to say we end
The heart-ache and the thousand natural shocks
That flesh is heir to, 'tis a consummation
Devoutly to be wish'd. To die, to sleep;
To sleep: perchance to dream: ay, there's the rub;
For in that sleep of death what dreams may come
When we have shuffled off this mortal coil,
Must give us pause: there's the respect
That makes calamity of so long life.

Hamlet Act III, Scene 1 lines 56–69

The What If? Game

Another type of parody is to play the 'What if . . .?' game. For example, what if Tony Blair had employed Edgar Allan Poe as the ghost writer for Volume One of his autobiography 'Tony Blair – The Early Years'?

Text 4 is what one A-Level English Language student wrote as an assignment in response to this question. It was written shortly after Labour's victory in the 1997 General Election in which Tony Blair became Prime Minister. It would help if you had read Poe's *The Tell-Tale Heart* before reading the next section. This is a story in which a madman commits a 'perfect' crime but is driven by his own conscience or insanity to admit to it after 'officers of the police' arrive to investigate suspected foul play but are satisfied nothing untoward has occurred.

TEXT 4

The Tell-Tale Electorate or *My Early Years* by Tony Blair – as told to E A Poe

I was, yes and still am, dreadfully nervous, but you cannot say that I am mad. Hearken, and note how I can tell the whole story in sound bites.

I do not know when first I conceived the idea but once formulated it haunted me day and night. I loved the idea of power. I loved the electorate. They had never rejected me. But it was this! Yes, it was this! They had voted Conservative for 18 years. Whenever I thought of this my blood ran cold and passions stiffened my backbone. Gradually, I determined to rid the country of Conservatives forever.

But how was I to do it? Before I could do the deed, I had to prepare my own party for government. To change its ideas would take time. And so I set about it slowly – very, very, very slowly, so that I would not disturb the sleep of Benn and Skinner.

You might imagine me to be mad! But mad persons know nothing – they do not even have a vote. You should have seen how cunningly I gathered support, with what honeyed words I flattered the voters. I never promised more than in the weeks leading up to the election.

Whenever the opportunity arose I appeared on *Question Time*, *P.M.* or *Today*. I was even prepared, if necessary, to appear on *Richard and Judy*. And so, smiling, I subtly pointed out the shortcomings of the Conservatives, seeking out for especial criticism their leader.

I did this for months. I was more than usually cautious in my dissembling, watching my personal ratings climb, but ever vigilant of avoiding a debacle such as the Sheffield rally of earlier times.

I checked the opinion polls punctiliously; listened avidly to the reports of focus groups but then, that night, I felt the full extent of my powers, my ascendance.

I entered Millbank and presently heard a groan. Not of pain or grief, but of exultation. Portillo had been defeated. With such feelings of joy as it is difficult to comprehend I received the congratulations of my acolytes. But even as I revelled in my magnificence I could feel a chilling presence, hear a haunting ululation indistinct in the ether.

I have told you that I was not mad, that my senses had become more acute. I knew the sound well. It was the sound of an electorate eager to have their wishes gratified.

At first I was unafraid. I had constructed the manifesto so cunningly, so seamlessly that none could detect a flaw. My spin doctors had so dextrously deflected criticism that no promises could be held against me, no trace of a policy could be discerned.

Yet the sound increased. It was a dull roar, like an animal in a truck awaiting slaughter across the English Channel. What could I do? Still, the Labour Party heard it not! I went on television to argue over trifles. During Prime Minister's Question Time I successfully evaded the questions of the party opposite. My supporters were satisfied. My smile convinced them that all was well. And still the noise increased. I undertook a national tour, a roadshow, debating in a high key with violent gesticulations, turning up the microphone to drown out the din. Yet the noise swelled, spreading and proliferating.

At length I could endure the tumult no more. I felt that I could no longer bear the opprobrium. I felt that I had to respond. I could hear the murmuring growing louder! Louder! Louder! Louder!

'Ingrates!' I shouted, 'Cry no more! I admit the deed! Do not turn your furious countenances upon me! I have buried Socialism under the floorboards!'

COMMENTARY   What might the writer of *The Tell-Tale Electorate* include in a commentary for A-Level?

The audience could be anyone with an interest in politics. Sixth form students of politics perhaps?

The piece was written as a parody but contains elements of pastiche in that words very close to Poe's in *The Tell-Tale Heart* are used. There is also satire in that the writer intends to comment on changes to Labour Party traditions. The structure is also a direct lift from Poe's tale.

Poe was a horror writer who uses a semantic group connected with the genre. In the parody the writer uses similar words and phrases. Included are words such as: dreadfully, haunted, my blood ran cold, passions, mad, chilling presence, endure and baleful.

To point the political aspects of the parody, words from that field are employed. Neologisms (new words or phrases which have recently entered the language) such as sound bite and spin doctor add to the modernity of the piece while a more traditional vocabulary includes electorate, policy, manifesto and socialism.

Poe writes in a florid style, using an elevated vocabulary. This is imitated in the use of words such as dissembling, ululations, punctiliously, exultations and countenances.

The original story is written in a staccato style meant to indicate the mental turmoil of the narrator. This is achieved by including a number of short, simple sentences and the liberal use of exclamation marks.

This, of course, does not constitute a full commentary. It is intended to indicate some of the areas the writer could consider when he comes to evaluate his own work.

Pastiche

Read the extract from *Pride and Prejudice*:
   a analyse Jane Austen's style; and then
   b write a passage of your own in imitation
      of that style.

If you need further guidance in analysing
an author's style, you should consult
Language and Style, a further book in this
series.

TEXT 5

It is a truth universally acknowledged that a single man in possession of a good fortune, must be in want of a wife.

However little known the feelings or views of such a man may be on his first entering a neighbourhood, this truth is so well fixed in the minds of the surrounding families, that he is considered as the rightful property of some one or other of their daughters.

'My dear Mr Bennet,' said his lady to him one day, 'have you heard that Netherfield Park is let at last?'

Mr Bennet replied that he had not.

'But it is,' returned she; 'for Mrs Long has just been here, and she told me all about it.'

Mr Bennet made no answer.

'Do not you want to know who has taken it?' cried his wife impatiently.

'You want to tell me, and I have no objection to hearing it.'

This was invitation enough.

'Why, my dear, you must know, Mrs Long says that Netherfield is taken by a young man of large fortune from the north of England; that he came down on Monday in a chaise and four to see the place, and was so much delighted with it that he agreed with Mr Morris immediately; that he is to take possession before Michaelmas, and some of his servants are to be in the house by the end of next week.'

'What is his name?'

'Bingley.'

'Is he married or single?'

'Oh! Single, my dear, to be sure! A single man of large fortune; four or five thousand a year. What a fine thing for our girls!'

'How so? How can it affect them?'

'My dear Mr Bennet,' replied his wife, 'how can you be so tiresome! You must know that I am thinking of his marrying one of them.'

Pride and Prejudice – Chapter 1

Don't think that you have to limit yourself to novels. Poetry offers many opportunities for parody and pastiche. On the Internet there is a website devoted to Spam, the famous tinned meat.

One contributor wrote a paper on the importance of Spam to Western European literature which included Andrew Marvell's 'To his Unsatisfactory Packed Lunch' which began:

Had we but Spam enough and time
This sandwich, lady, were no crime . . .

and is based on Marvell's original poem *To His Coy Mistress* which opened:

Had we but world enough, and time,
This coyness, lady, were no crime . . .

Coleridge too received the 'Spam' treatment:

In Xanadu did Kubla Khan
A tastebud overload decree
And Alf, the local grocer, ran
Through aisle on aisle of pinkest Spam . . .

Compare it to the original from *Kubla Khan*

In Xanadu did Kubla Khan
A stately pleasure dome decree,
Where Alph, the sacred river ran,
Through caverns measureless to man . . .

Even nursery rhymes were 'spammed':

Mary had a tin of Spam,
She used it as a seat, it
Doubled as her evening meal,
'cause later on she'd eat it . . .

ACTIVITY 3

Choose a poem you know well and borrow its rhyme scheme and metre for comic effect. You could, of course 'spam' it!

To produce a parody, pastiche or satire you should consider:

■ the form of the original;

■ the main stylistic features which will enable the reader to recognise exactly what it is you are parodying or satirising; and

■ your audience's familiarity (or lack of it) with the original or model.

Satire

Satire differs from parody in a number of ways, some of them quite subtle. Though a satirist might incidentally entertain an audience, that is not always his first intention. Satire, according to Dr Samuel Johnson's dictionary published in 1755 is 'a poem in which wickedness or folly is censured'.

A satirist sets out to tell the truth as he sees it while laughing at, or joking about, serious things.

Satire's existence as a separate thread of literature appears to date from the 5th century BC and the works of the Athenian poet Aristophanes, who satirised famous people of his day using abuse and ridicule in his plays. Though his reason for writing was his love of Greece, Aristophanes attacked many people of high repute. In *Clouds*, he presented Socrates as a silly, interfering fool and in *Knights*, he presented the Athenian general, Cleon as a vulgar rabble-rouser. He also examined the oppression of women in *Lysistrata*.

Before Aristophanes another Greek satirist, Hipponax, was apparently so cruel in his invective that several of his targets committed suicide. Perhaps this is taking satire a bit too far.

The Roman satirists claimed to be giving warnings or exposing scandals. In the 1st century BC the Roman poet, Horace, did this in a witty, civilised way, apparently laughing at the foibles he was criticising.

With the spread of Christianity satire lost ground as a literary form. Though some strong lectures were delivered from the pulpit to criticise the wicked and foolish, these did not have the 'laughter behind the truth' of the Greek and Roman satirists.

In the 14th century Geoffrey Chaucer satirised the institution of marriage from a woman's point of view in *The Wife of Bath's Prologue.* Chaucer's character delivers a monologue in the tradition of the classical satirists. Chaucer is a subtle writer who puts into the mouth of his creation a feminist diatribe (a bitter presentation of an argument against someone or something) while at the same time making the reader have some sympathy for her five previous husbands.

In 1725 Jonathan Swift published *Gulliver's Travels.* Though it has appeared in many re-written versions as a children's story, in the original it is a satire on many of the issues of the day. Swift called his book, 'a direct, plain and bitter satire against the innumerable follies and corruption in law, politics, learning, morals and religion' and wrote that, 'The chief end I propose to myself in all my labours is to vex the world rather than divert it.'

In the first section of Gulliver's voyages he is washed up after a shipwreck on the shores of Lilliput, the land of the little people. There are many references in this account to contemporary English politics. The religious dispute between Protestants and Catholics over a period of 100 years is referred to in Swift's account of the squabble between the Big-Endians and their opponents over which end of a egg should be cracked prior to eating it.

Swift also describes the methods by which politicians gain advancement in Lilliput. They have to show their skill at jumping over or creeping under sticks and dancing on ropes. In 1725 George I had revived the Order of the Bath and Prime Minister Walpole began a policy of rewarding his cronies with honours. Here is Swift's description of the rope dancing needed to succeed in gaining this honour.

TEXT 6

The Emperor had a mind one Day to entertain me with several of the Country Shows; wherein they exceed all Nations I have known, both for Dexterity and Magnificence. I was diverted with none so much as that of the Rope-Dancers, performed upon a slender white Thread, extended about two Foot, and twelve Inches from the Ground. Upon which, I shall desire Liberty, with the Reader's Patience, to enlarge a little.

This Diversion is only practised by those Persons, who are Candidates for great Employments, and high Favour, at Court. They are trained in this Art from their Youth, and are not always of noble Birth, or liberal Education. When a great Office is vacant, either by Death or Disgrace, (which often happens) five or six of those Candidates petition the Emperor to entertain his Majesty and the Court with a Dance on the Rope; and whoever jumps the highest without falling, succeeds in the Office. Very often the chief Ministers themselves are commanded to shew their Skill, and to convince the Emperor that they have not lost their Faculty.

Swift also uses Gulliver's own snobbery to make fun of the class structure and morality of his own time. Gulliver had saved Lilliput from impending invasion by the neighbouring empire of Blefescu by towing its war fleet into harbour in Lilliput. For this service the Emperor had given him the title of Nardac, the highest title of honour in Lilliput. Gulliver is extremely pleased by this honour, especially when he feels he has to defend the honour of a lady who is rumoured 'to have come privately to my lodging.' The farcical idea of a dalliance between himself and a woman only 6 inches in height does not appear to Gulliver or the lady's detractors.

Swift had what some critics refer to as 'cloacal concerns' (to do with urine and faeces). He was also fanatical about personal hygiene as this extract shows.

TEXT 7

[*At this point Gulliver is in Brobdingnag where he is tiny compared to the inhabitants*]
The Maids of Honour often invited Glumdalclitch [*the daughter of the farmer who had discovered Gulliver on his arrival in Brobdingnag*] to their Apartments, and desired she would bring me along with her, on Purpose to have the Pleasure of seeing and touching me. They would often strip me naked from Top to Toe, and lay me at full Length in their Bosoms; wherewith I was much disgusted; because, to say the Truth, a very offensive Smell came from their Skins, which I do not mention or intend to the Disadvantage of those Ladies, for whom I have all Manner of Respect: But, I conceive that my Sense was more acute in Proportion to my Littleness; and that those illustrious Persons were no more disagreeable to their Lover, or to each other, than People of the Quality are with us in England. And, after all, I found their natural Smell was much more supportable than when they used Perfumes, under which I immediately swooned away.

Let's summarise what we've seen of satire so far. Writers of satire may use:

- brutally direct language
- nauseating imagery
- elements of parody
- serious subject matters
- topicality
- irony
- paradox.

Modern satire

In the 20th century, satire became extremely popular again, especially in the late 1950s and 1960s. The modern satirists wished to question the established order and used humour to deride the government of the day. Dr Jonathan Miller has suggested that the values of the 19th century with its insistence on good manners and the 'philistine values of an industrial elite' had led to the blunting of satire. Now it was back in the material of performers at Peter Cook's *Establishment Club*, in the magazine *Private Eye* and on television shows such as *That Was The Week That Was*.

Satire tends to gain popularity as society becomes settled along fixed lines. The satirists of the 1950s and 1960s were reacting to what they saw as a government of a privileged class – the Conservative government which was in power from 1951–64.

After many years of Margaret Thatcher's government a new generation of satirists emerged. These included Ben Elton, Alexei Sayle and the writers and actors on television's *Spitting Image*.

As it is often topical in nature, much of the satire of the 1960s doesn't travel across time well, though a sketch written by Marty Feldman and

John Law on the British class system still has a point to make. The point was made more effective by the respective heights of the performers. John Cleese at 6 feet 5 inches, represented the upper class, Ronnie Barker at 5 feet 8 inches represented the middle class and Ronnie Corbett at 5 feet 1 inch represented the working class.

TEXT 8

Class

Cleese: I look down on him [indicating Barker] because I am upper-class.

Barker: I look up to him [indicating Cleese] because he is upper-class; but I look down on him [indicating Corbett] because he is lower class. I am middle-class.

Corbett: I know my place. I look up to them both. But I don't look up to him [Barker] as much as I look up to him [Cleese], because he has got innate breeding.

Cleese: I have got innate breeding, but I haven't got any money. So sometimes I look up [bending knees to do so] to him [Barker].

Barker: I still look up to him [Cleese] because although I have money, I am vulgar. But I am not as vulgar as him [Corbett], so I still look down on him [Corbett].

Corbett: I know my place. I look up to them both; but while I am poor, I am honest, industrious and trustworthy. Had I the inclination, I could look down on them. But I don't.

Barker: We all know our place, but what do we get out of it?

Cleese: I get a feeling of superiority over them.

Barker: I get a feeling of inferiority from him [Cleese], but a feeling of superiority over him [Corbett].

Corbett: I get a pain in the neck.

Peter Cook invented a character whom he later named E. L. Wisty. In this character he would improvise on an issue of the day. In this monologue, Wisty comments on the age of judges and compares this to what happens to miners of retirement age.

TEXT 9

E. L. Wisty's Monologue

Yes, I could have been a judge but I never had the Latin, never had the Latin for the judging. I just never had sufficient of it to get through the rigorous judging exams. They're noted for their rigour. People come staggering out saying, 'My God, what a rigorous exam – '. And so I became a miner instead. A coal miner. I managed to get through the mining exams – they're not very rigorous, they only ask you one question, they say, 'Who are you?' and I got 75% on that –

Of course, it's quite interesting work, getting hold of lumps of coal all day, it's quite interesting. Because the coal was made in a very unusual way. You see, God blew all the trees down. He didn't just say 'let's have some coal'. As he could have done, He had all the right contacts. No, he got this great wind thing going, you see, and blew down all the trees, then, over a period of three million years, He changed it into coal, gradually over a period of three million years so it wasn't noticeable to the average passer-by. It was all part of the scheme, but people at the time did not see it that way. People under the trees did not say, 'Hurrah – coal in three million years,' no – they said, 'Oh dear, oh dear, trees falling on us – that's the last thing we want', and of course their wish was granted.

The trouble with it is the people. I am not saying you get a load of riffraff down the mine. I am not saying that, I am just saying we had a load of riffraff down *my* mine. Very boring conversationalists, extremely boring, all they talk about is what goes on in the mine. Extremely boring. If you were searching for a word to describe the conversations that go on down the mine, boring would spring to your lips. – 'Oh God! They're very boring'. If ever you want to hear things like: 'Hello, I've found a bit of coal. Have you really? Yes, no doubt about it, this black substance is coal all right. Jolly good, the very thing we're looking for.'

Whoops. Did you notice I suddenly went whoops? It's an impediment I got from being down the mine. 'Cause one day I was walking along in the dark when I came across the body of a dead pit pony. Whoops, I went in surprise, and ever since then I've been going whoops and that's another reason I couldn't be a judge, because I might have been up there all regal, sentencing away, 'I sentence you to whoops', and you see, the trouble is under English law that would have to stand. So all in all I'd rather have been a judge than a miner.

And what is more, being a miner, as soon as you are too old and tired and sick and stupid to do the job properly, you have to go. Well, the very opposite applies with the judges. So all in all I would rather have been a judge than a miner – Because I've always been after the trappings of great luxury you see, I really, really have. But all I've got hold of are the trappings of great poverty. I've got hold of the wrong load of trappings, and a rotten load of trappings they are too, ones I could've very well done without.

Private Eye magazine carried a comic strip written by Barry Humphries before he became better known as Dame Edna Everage. His target in *The Adventures of Barry McKenzie* was what he saw as 'the smug complacency' of the Australian community and he created McKenzie, a vulgar working class character who thinks he is enlightened and educated but is, in fact, easily shocked and ignorant. This strip is also interesting for its use of Australian vernacular – particularly when dealing with bodily functions and vomiting, linking it directly to Swiftian satire.

In this example Humphries also attacks the pretensions of the art world.

TEXT 10

Terry Pratchett, creator of the Discworld series has a very light touch with his satire. In this extract from 'Jingo' (jingoism is exaggerated pride in one's country), Sergeant Colon and Corporal Nobbs of the Ankh-Morpork Watch (Anhk-Morpork is one of the major cities of the Discworld and with a few exceptions, the Watch is not noted for the intelligence of its officers who are direct descendants of Dogberry and Verges in Shakespeare's *Much Ado About Nothing*) are discussing the imminent war with Klatch (for Klatch read any Middle Eastern or Asian state) as they are out on patrol.

TEXT 11

Extract from 'Jingo'

A familiar creak made them look up. A Klatchian's head was swinging in the breeze.
'Fancy a pint?' said Sergeant Colon. 'Big Angie brews up some that's a treat.'
'Better not, sarge. Mr. Vimes [Commander of the Watch] is in a bit of a mood.'
Colon sighed. 'You're right.'

Nobby looked up at the head again. It was wooden. It had been repainted many times over the centuries. The Klatchian was smiling very happily for someone who'd never have to buy a shirt ever again.

'The Klatchian's Head. My grandad said his grandad remembered when it was still the real one,' Colon said. 'Of course, it was about the size of a walnut by then.'

'Bit ... nasty, sticking up a bloke's head for a pub sign,' said Nobby.

'No, Nobby. Spoils of war, right? Some bloke come back from one of the wars with a souvenir, stuck it on a pole and opened a pub. The Klatchian's Head. Teach 'em not to do it again.'

'I used to get into enough trouble just for nicking boots,' said Nobby.

'More robust times, Nobby.'

'You ever met a Klatchian, sarge?' said Nobby, as they began to pace the length of the quiet street. 'I mean one of the wild ones.'

'Well, no ... but you know what? They're allowed three wives! That's criminal that is.'

'Yeah, 'cos here's me and I ain't got one,' said Nobby.

'And they eat funny grub. Curry and that.'

Nobby gave this some thought. 'Like ... we do, when we're on late duty.'

'Weelll, yerss – but they don't do it properly – '

'You mean runny ear-wax yellow with peas and currants in, like your mum used to do?'

'Right! You poke around as much as you like in a Klatchian curry and you won't find a single piece of swede.'

'And I heard they eat sheep's eyeballs, too,' said Nobby, international gastra-gnome.

'Right again.'

'Not decent ordinary stuff like lambs' fry or sweetbreads, then?'

'That's ... right.'

Colon felt he was being got at in some way.

'Look, Nobby, when all's said and done they ain't the right colour, and that's an end to it.'

'Good job you found out, Fred!' said Nobby, so cheerfully that Sergeant Colon was almost sure he meant it.

'Well, it's obvious,' he conceded.

'Er ... what is the right colour?' said Nobby.

'White, of course!'

'Not brick-red, then? 'Cos you – '

'Are you winding me up, Corporal Nobbs?'

' 'Course not, sarge. So ... what colour am I?'

That caused Sergeant Colon to think. You could have found, somewhere on Corporal Nobbs, a shade appropriate to every climate on the disc and a few found only in specialist medical books.

'White's ... white's a state of, you know ... mind,' he said. 'It's like ... doing an honest day's work for an honest day's pay, that sort of thing. And washing regular.'

'Not lazing around, sort of thing.'

'Right.'

'Or ... like ... working all hours like Goriff does.'

'Nobby – '

'And you never see those kids of his with dirty clo-'

'Nobby, you're just trying to get me going, right? You know we're better'n Klatchians. Otherwise, what's the point? Anyway, if we're going to fight 'em, you could get locked up for going around talking treachery.'

Pratchett's take on prejudice is quite subtle. Sergeant Colon can't help feeling as he does about Klatch and Klatchians as public feeling has been stirred up against them and to present a reasonable case, as Corporal Nobbs does, for there not being any real differences between the inhabitants of Anhk-Morpork and Klatch would be seen as unpatriotic.

ACTIVITY 4

Choose an issue of the day and, having spotted the possible follies behind it, attempt to write a short satirical piece that highlights the 'truth behind the laughter'.

Here are some suggestions:

- There is a growing trend to call hospitals 'Health Parks'. If this were to be developed, would a serious operation be seen as the ultimate white-knuckle ride? Could surgeons try to out-do each other in offering attractions as theme parks do? It is possible to see jousting at the theme park, Camelot. How about open-heart surgery as a spectator sport – with volunteers from the audience to pass the scalpels?

- The supermarket chain, Somerfield, sponsored the name-tags of politicians, journalists etc at the Labour Party Conference of 1998. Could sponsors influence a policy? Perhaps the makers of locks could back a policy of imprisoning more offenders for trivial reasons? Would makers of slimming foods put money into a campaign to combat obesity?

- We are already seeing fast-food chains offering vouchers to schools to reward performance, good attendance etc. How might this affect lessons on nutrition?

If you think about it, you'll find many potential subjects for satire.

2 Radio, Television and Film

One of the most popular forms of writing for A-Level English Language is the script. However, problems can arise when students, who are extremely visually literate because of their familiarity with television and film, attempt to write for radio, which is a sound medium.

If scriptwriting were an easy form to master there would be more people successfully earning their living in a potentially lucrative business.

Lend Me Your Ears – Radio Drama

It is best to study the layout, technical language and other conventions of the form before starting work on a script.

Many students attempt to produce scripts without this preparatory research and it shows! Drama is a staple of Radio 4 in Britain, though plays do appear on other networks occasionally. Radio 4 transmits series such as *Thirty Minute Theatre* and *The Afternoon Play*, as well as the world's longest-running soap opera *The Archers*. From time to time surprises do crop up. For instance, *The Adventures of Superman* was broadcast on Radio 4 in a late evening slot.

The fact that radio is a sound-only medium gives writers a degree of freedom not allowed to writers for film and television unless they are writing for a big budget film. Radio can move the listener from a tropical rainforest to a car assembly plant to a spacecraft orbiting the earth either by sound effects or with a well crafted line of dialogue.

In *The Adventures of Superman*, listeners were invited to accept that a buzzing noise represented Superman's heat vision as he was having a shave. They understood without question that the buzzing was a sound representation of beams emanating from Superman's eyes! The change in role from the heroic Superman to his nervous, prissy Clark Kent persona was suggested by a change in pitch of the actor's voice. A deep, resonant tone for Superman and a lighter, hesitant tone for Clark.

In a scene during which Clark and his colleague, Lois Lane, are supposed to be flying by helicopter to a reception on a large yacht owned by Superman's enemy, Lex Luthor, the actors shouted over the sound effects of rotor blades and distorted voices over the helicopter's radio. As they approached the yacht a comment was made to the effect that it looked as big as the QE2. The pilot replied,

Considerably larger, actually.

This is a skilful way of giving visual detail through sounds and words. A simple formula for the aspiring radio script writer is:

Words + Sounds + Music = Radio

ACTIVITY 5

1 Listen to a short radio drama and make a list of the techniques used. Take particular note of the variety of voices, use of sound effects, the way dialogue is used to further the plot and the way scene changes and the passage of time is signalled.

2 In groups, discuss your lists and compare the techniques you have noted.

Audience

All writers have to consider the audience, but the writer for radio has to give perhaps more attention to them than writers for the other media. The broadcast story or play has to be structured extremely carefully as once the actor has delivered the words the listener cannot go back and re-read a complex paragraph as they could with a printed text, or re-run mentally a scene just watched on television.

A further thing to remember is that though some radio programmes command an audience of millions, that audience tends to be comprised of individuals; individuals probably doing something else at the same time, such as driving a car, doing the ironing or cooking. This makes radio an intensely intimate medium.

Characters in a radio play are not seen. This might seem too obvious to state, but it means that the writer must distinguish between the characters in some way, so listeners don't get confused. One way of doing this is to create a range of characters of different gender, age or nationalities. A point to consider here is that while accent is a useful marker, it is much easier for the writer to state that a certain character has a specific regional accent and trust the producer to cast an actor who can deliver the goods rather than attempt to write the accent phonetically.

Another hint to check whether your script is working is to cover the names of your characters and see if you can recognise them by their speech patterns. Shakespeare's Dogberry in *Much Ado About Nothing* is instantly recognisable by the way he mangles language. In a more modern example, *Coronation Street*'s Fred Elliot can be recognised by his habit of repeating phrases and his initiating signal of 'Ah say . . .'.

If you carry out this test on your own script you might spot some lines which aren't forwarding the plot, revealing character or creating atmosphere. Cut them!

Radio conventions

You should be aware of the conventions of radio when writing. These are the clues in the script, which let the listener know, for example, who the characters are, what their relationship is. You also need to follow the conventions of presentation and layout in a radio script:

- all pages are numbered and each section of dialogue on the page is also numbered
- the speaker's name is capitalised and to the left of the lines
- directions regarding location and sound effects are centred, in capitals and underlined.

There may be minor variations on this model but if you keep to these guidelines you will have a script that is clear and easy to follow.

JOHN:	(Shouting) I need a word now, Sarah!
SARAH:	(Distant – from bedroom) Can't it wait, Dad?
JOHN:	No it can't! Get down here this minute!

A BEDROOM DOOR IS SLAMMED LOUDLY AND HEAVY FOOTSTEPS ARE HEARD AS SARAH COMES DOWNSTAIRS

SARAH:	(Heavily, resigned) Okay, Dad, what is it?

The example above shows family relationships. Sarah refers to the male speaker as 'Dad' twice and it is apparent from his speech that 'Dad' is older than, or has some authority over Sarah. It is as easy to demonstrate status relationships.

CONSTABLE:	There's a woman at the desk wanting to report the loss of her rhinoceros, Sarge.
SERGEANT:	Don't just stand there, lad. Have you got a description yet?
CONSTABLE:	Yes, Sarge. About 5 feet 4 inches tall wearing a pink trouser suit and pearls.
SERGEANT:	Can't be many rhinoceri dressed like that – we shouldn't have much trouble finding it.

If the signals are handled badly the results can be farcical. In the extract below the writer has taken the need to tell the listeners what is going on to extremes.

TEXT 12

A KEY TURNS IN A LOCK AND A DOOR OPENS

JOHN:	Darling, I'm home. I'm really shattered. That 20 minute drive from my office in the city of Riverport – that thriving metropolis which was founded by Alfred the Great – to our ultra-modern semi here in the leafy suburb of Applegate gets worse every day.
JANE:	Poor darling. Here's your gin and tonic. (TINKLE OF BOTTLE ON GLASS) But I've got some news that will cheer you up. You know our daughter.
JOHN:	You mean Jade, our cute tousle-haired 6 year old whom I can see out in the garden playing with Jasper, our King Charles spaniel. (SOUND OF A SMALL DOG YAPPING IN DISTANCE)
JANE:	Yes, that daughter. Well Mr Holmes, our 62 year old neighbour who lost a leg in the Korean War, has made her a tree house. He's putting it up in the apple tree now.
JOHN:	That could be rather dangerous for a man of his age.

SOUNDS OF BRANCHES BREAKING, LEAVES SWISHING AND A LOUD THUD

JOHN:	I told you so. He's only gone and fallen out of the tree!

ACTIVITY 6

1 Rewrite the script so that it is more realistic and works for radio.
2 Discuss with a partner the techniques you used. How did you get all the information across to the audience without it sounding staged?

At the other end of the scale, would-be radio script writers who haven't done their preparatory work and are more familiar with television conventions sometimes give descriptions which are visual. While this might help with any background sounds or acoustics it does not assist the listener. For example:

TEXT 13

IT IS MIDDAY. JOHN IS SITTING ON A DRY STONE WALL,
LOOKING AT HIS MAP AND TRYING TO DECIDE WHICH WAY
TO GO. THE SUN IS SHINING BRIGHTLY AND HE IS WEARING
A BRIGHTLY COLOURED JACKET.

When you feel you have a firm grasp of radio production techniques, and you are confident that you can layout a script in a way which makes it clear that it is a script for radio the next stages to follow are common to all types of scripting or story writing.

Writing a synopsis of the plot, character sketches and, if applicable, a list of locations, will give you a series of reference points while you're constructing the script and will give you some ready-made material for inclusion in your commentary, especially if you make changes as the script develops. Be prepared for your characters to hi-jack the script or the story to take turns you didn't plan when you first began work on it. If this happens don't fight it, instead, 'go with the flow'. It's likely your story will be the better for it.

Writer N. J. Warburton suggests that at least one of the characters in any drama should have a secret. Think of Macbeth's secret murder of Duncan and the strain it puts him under, or the mother in Willy Russell's *Blood Brothers* who is forced by poverty to give one of her new-born twins to a rich, childless couple. In Warburton's whimsical radio comedy *The Messenger*, a young, not very-well educated man named Albert drifts into a job in the vast offices of a publishing company. It is 1911 and the offices of Quinn and Lundy are in London. Albert falls under the influence of the lift operator, Mr Drummer. The author's notes describe Drummer in this way:

DRUMMER: forty to fifty; the lift operator – a direct London voice.

Drummer has a secret, one which he reveals to Albert when he feels that Albert is becoming too friendly with Mr Trounce, the lift operator on the other side of the building. Drummer does not approve of Mr Trounce because, 'He has no curiosity. He doesn't want to know anything.'

In this extract, Drummer learns that Albert has not only spoken to Trounce but got him to respond. Albert has taken to eating his lunch in Drummer's lift. Drummer stops the lift between floors while they eat. In this extract we pick up the action on page 40, the 13th utterance.

TEXT 14

13	ALBERT:	I wanted to see if I could get him to talk. And he did.
14	DRUMMER:	You're a dark horse you are.
15	ALBERT:	In fact, he came down the corridor with me. He didn't say very much but …
16	DRUMMER:	You mean he left his lift?
17	ALBERT:	Yes.
18	DRUMMER:	You're a fool, Albert. I've told you before, it's a dangerous game to tempt a man out of his lift even a man like Trounce.

–41–

1	ALBERT:	Sorry, Mr Drummer. I didn't think you'd …
2	DRUMMER:	Didn't think. You didn't think. That's your trouble, Albert: you never think.
3	ALBERT:	I know. (Pause) Aren't you eating?
4	DRUMMER:	I am, in a manner of speaking, yes. (TAKING OUT HIS PARCEL) Although I begin to wonder if I ought to after what you've just told me.
5	ALBERT:	It's that parcel you had.
6	DRUMMER:	It is.
7	ALBERT:	Oh yes. I forgot about that. You said to remind you.
8	DRUMMER:	But your head was too full of the wonderful doings of the great Trounce.
9	ALBERT:	No, honestly. I just forgot. What is it, Mr Drummer?
10	DRUMMER:	(UNWRAPPING THE PARCEL) A cardboard box. And inside …
11	ALBERT:	Crikey. Lightbulbs.
12	DRUMMER:	Correct, Albert. Old lightbulbs to be precise.
13	ALBERT:	What are they for?
14	DRUMMER:	Wait and you shall see.

(SLIGHT PAUSE FOLLOWED BY THE SOUND OF DRUMMER CRUNCHING UP A LIGHTBULB. HE FINISHES IT AND THERE IS A STUNNED SILENCE)

–42–

1	ALBERT:	(Quietly) Crikey.
2	DRUMMER:	Well?
3	ALBERT:	What did you do that for? You could kill yourself. Broken glass and I don't know what.
4	DRUMMER:	Little bits of wire. Makes a change from bread and cheese, Albert.
5	ALBERT:	But … did you swallow it?
6	DRUMMER:	Of course I did. You saw me, didn't you? It's no trick, lad. I eat lightbulbs. Not very often but they're not all that easy to get hold of.
7	ALBERT:	Why?
8	DRUMMER:	Because most of the lighting round here is still gas …
9	ALBERT:	I mean, why do you do it?
10	DRUMMER:	Ah. Good question. Not for the nourishment. There's very little nourishment in a lightbulb as far as I can tell. I don't think much of it goes into the system. No, it's more the mystery of the thing that makes me do it.
11	ALBERT:	The mystery?
12	DRUMMER:	Yes. It is a mystery, isn't it?
13	ALBERT:	Oh yes.
14	DRUMMER:	I mean, you've never seen it before, I should think.

–43–

| 1 | ALBERT: | Never. |
| 2 | DRUMMER: | I discovered it by accident. I've always had what you might call a strong constitution although that's never led to any special craving for broken glass. But I happened to be in my little workroom one day with a lightbulb in my mouth. I was standing on a chair, you see, trying to screw the old bulb out. I stumbled from the chair, inadvertently shut my mouth and, before I knew what was happening, I'd done quite a lot of crunching and had one accidental swallow. I lay there for some little time and I thought, 'This is it, Drummer, you've met your end now,' and it occurred to me that it was an odd way to go. In fact, I was wondering how to explain it to my sister who's a bit suspicious of lightbulbs anyway. Of course, I didn't see the senselessness of that thought because I was in a state of trepidation at the time. My main |

concern was the electricity. It's a powerful and invisible thing, you know, Albert – but as the seconds ticked by I could tell I'd survived the threat. And after that the broken lightbulb didn't seem so bad.

3 ALBERT: So now you do it on purpose?

4 DRUMMER: Well, it sort of developed. But, as I say, it was the mystery that attracted me to the idea. Man was not made to eat lightbulbs and yet here was I doing just that. Man was not made to glide upwards and downwards without the use of his legs and here was I doing that very thing every day. What a marvel man is, I thought. There's no limit to what he might do.

–44–

1 DRUMMER: So I eat lightbulbs to demonstrate man's forward push towards his next adventure. It's also made me quite popular, of course. Several of the senior people have asked for a demonstration.

2 ALBERT: You amaze me, Mr Drummer. I never thought I'd see a man do such a thing.

3 DRUMMER: You didn't see old Trounce eating lightbulbs?

4 ALBERT: Oh no.

5 DRUMMER: You must profit by it, lad. I don't suspend the lift like this so that any Tom, Dick or Harry can see me eating lightbulbs. I do it for the sake of the few who will understand.

6 ALBERT: And you think I can understand?

7 DRUMMER: Of course. You have a questing spirit. And you haven't been ground down by this place yet. There's hope in you, Albert.

ACTIVITY 7

In small groups, discuss the following questions:

1 How is Drummer shown to be the older, dominant speaker in this extract?

2 How is Drummer's jealousy over Albert's contact with his rival lift operator, Mr Trounce, shown?

3 How does Albert's speech show him to be the younger, more hesitant of the two speakers?

4 What piece of information does Albert directly reveal in his speech which is necessary to the listener's complete understanding of the action?

Writers also need to consider the number of words which go into a script. People normally talk at about 180 words per minute, but when you speak for emphasis this drops to nearer 130 wpm. Robin Cook, the Foreign Secretary at the time, addressed the House of Commons about an international crisis in 1998 and spoke at an average 135 wpm.

An actor in performance probably delivers the lines at the lower end of this 130–180 wpm scale for the sake of clarity. This is not to say that the writer of a 30 minute script has to produce 4000 words plus. The opening titles, closing credits and the times when sounds or pictures (according to the medium) tell the story will reduce that number considerably.

Another point to consider is that you are creating fictional speech. This differs from 'normal' speech almost as much as spoken language differs from written language.

You will have studied the difference between speech and writing as part of your A-Level course. You will have looked at topics such as formality, correctness, planning and spontaneity. You will have noted that spoken language is full of non-fluency features such as words and phrases being left out, syntax errors, anacoluthon (starting one sentence then changing the sentence topic halfway through), hesitation, filled and unfilled pauses.

Conversation also contains overlapping, phatic communion (the 'ums' and 'ahs' or gestures which reassure a speaker that we're listening), echoing and interruption.

However, in everyday conversation the brain acts as a filter, editing out all the features of spontaneous speech which would be very irritating if we were acutely aware of them.

This presents the writer with a problem. How can we write a script which is supposed to be realistic and naturalistic if we leave out those features which make spoken language so alive and immediate?

The answer is that to replicate 'normal' speech the scriptwriter places a few non-fluency features in the fictional speech – the odd false start, a couple of filled pauses or an overlapping sentence or two.

To sum up, as a scriptwriter you are creating an illusion which convinces the listeners or viewers that they are hearing real speakers.

ACTIVITY 8

Using a maximum of three speakers write a short scene set in:

  a a leisure centre; or
  b a hospital casualty department; or
  c a classroom.

Make sure that the location, characters and theme of the scene are all revealed in the dialogue, which should be as natural as you can make it. Try saying your words aloud to check that your script does sound like everyday speech.

Writing a television script

All the comments on planning before attempting to write for radio apply equally to writing for television. Modern television audiences are extremely visually literate and understand the medium almost instinctively. This leads to comments of the 'Did you see that on the box last night? Absolute rubbish! I could do better myself' variety.

But of course, for most people this simply isn't the case. Writing for television is a demanding and difficult task. However, if you study the medium, and learn what a script looks like, you at least have a chance to produce a competent script.

It would be difficult for you to write a full length play or even an episode from a soap opera (or a 'thrice-weekly continuing drama' as those involved in their production prefer to refer to them) because of the time available to you, to say nothing of having to keep within a word count.

You can, of course, write an extract from a longer work or a series of short scripts, perhaps as part of an advertising campaign or public information package.

Choose a short TV drama to watch. This might be an episode of your favourite soap, a situation comedy, a programme like *The Bill* or a short play. Watch it as an active rather than a passive viewer, making notes on the following questions:

1 How many scenes are there?
2 What is the structure of the programme?
3 Where have the writers put the 'hooks', the teasing comments or hints of a revelation about a character or plot development that will make you want to continue watching? On the commercial channels these will usually come just before an advertising break.
4 How long is the average scene?
5 How many characters appear in each scene?
6 How many words are spoken in a scene?

What does a TV script look like?

Very roughly speaking, one page of television script equals 40 seconds of screen time if you are using the format suggested here.

Scene headings, which give details of where and when the action is taking place are always presented in capitals. These headings always include whether the scene takes place indoors or outdoors, (presented as INT or EXT) and the time of day. It is usually enough to indicate DAY or NIGHT.

Again, spacing is important. Always use double spacing between headings and dialogue, or leave two lines if you are handwriting your script. The main reason for this spacing is ease of understanding for the reader. In a television script the left hand page is left blank.

A beginner should not give too many camera directions. There will be times when you want to suggest a close up (CU) or a long shot (LS) but as a general rule you should leave this sort of detail to the director.

Similarly, unless there is a very good reason, you should not tell the actors how to deliver the lines. A very good reason would be that a particular tone or emphasis was vital to the dramatic impetus of the script.

You will probably only need the following terms in your script:

■ FADE IN – used at the start of a script
■ FADE OUT – used at the end of a script
■ CUT TO – used at the end of a scene
■ VO (Voice over) – used for narration, or when a character who is off-screen speaks to others who are seen. (This is sometimes referred to as OOV or Out of Vision)
■ POV (Point of view) – used when the camera is supposed to be looking through the eyes of the character who is speaking.

The following is an extract from a television play entitled *Calais in the Morning*. In the two scenes which follow, the three male characters are in a motorway service area. Paul and Dave are close friends. They regularly make the drive from their northern home town to Calais in order to stock up with beer and wine. On this occasion they are accompanied by Chris, Dave's brother-in-law. It is Chris' first time on the trip and he is only along because Dave's wife has insisted. There has been a festering argument between Paul and Chris, partly because they are travelling in Paul's ancient van and Chris has been sitting in the back being bounced about. He has tried unsuccessfully to get some sleep and is feeling fed-up and fractious.

TEXT 15

SCENE FIFTEEN   EXT   NIGHT

THE RESTAURANT AREA OF THE SERVICES. THE THREE ARE SITTING AT A TABLE. THERE HAS OBVIOUSLY BEEN AN ARGUMENT. THE CONVERSATION IS HEATED.

PAUL:	I'm getting really brassed off with your sarky comments.
CHRIS:	It's a joke, okay?
PAUL:	Well it isn't funny!
DAVE:	Let's all drop it, shall we?
CHRIS (TO DAVE):	Why can't he take a joke?
PAUL:	I can … when it's funny.
CHRIS:	I think the whole thing's stupid anyway
PAUL:	If it's stupid, why are you tagging along?
CHRIS:	'Cause I was badgered into it, that's why!
DAVE:	You've been badgered! Who by?

PAUSE, THEN THEY SAY TOGETHER

DAVE/CHRIS:	Julia!
CHRIS:	Yeah, well, she's been acting weird recently.
PAUL:	That's what women do. And I should know, I married four of them.
CHRIS:	What??? At once?
PAUL:	Don't be daft. One after the other. And they're all weird, even Joanne. And she's great.
CHRIS:	So, you've been married four times, and you can write off evolution, progress and feminism in one phrase, 'Women are weird'.
PAUL (DEFENSIVELY):	Well, they're not like us are they?
CHRIS:	So tell me … is this hypothesis based on empirical proof or is it merely a piece of whimsy?
PAUL (PUZZLED):	Wha …? Look you! Just because you've got an education and know some long words, it doesn't give you the right to take the piss.
CHRIS:	Doesn't it? You're a neanderthal, Paul.

PAUL GETS UP AS IF TO THUMP CHRIS. DAVE PUSHES HIM DOWN INTO HIS SEAT.

DAVE:	Button it, the pair of you. Shut up Chris and you … (TO PAUL) just calm down. People are looking at us.
PAUL:	Well I'm sick of him and his comments.
CHRIS:	I'm going to the gents.

HE GETS UP AND WALKS OFF. PAUL GLOWERS AT HIS BACK THEN SEEMS TO MAKE A DECISION.

PAUL:	Come on.

HE STANDS UP AND PULLS AT DAVE'S ARM.

DAVE:	I haven't finished my coffee yet.
PAUL:	Leave it. Come on.

DAVE DRAINS HIS CUP AS PAUL DRAGS HIM AWAY AND THEY EXIT.

CUT TO:

SCENE SIXTEEN   EXT   NIGHT

WE SEE CHRIS COME OUT OF THE RESTAURANT.

CUT TO CU AS HE REACTS.

CUT TO POV SHOT OF EMPTY SPACE WHERE THE VAN WAS PARKED.
CUT TO CU OF CHRIS' GUITAR IN THE PARKING SPACE.
CUT TO MED. SHOT AS CHRIS (LOOKING DAZED) WANDERS OVER TO PICK UP HIS GUITAR.
THERE IS A MESSAGE IN CHALK ON THE TARMAC.
CUT TO CHRIS' POV AGAIN AS HE READS THE MESSAGE. IT SAYS 'COULDN'T WAIT! CROSS
BRIDGE. WE'LL PICK YOU UP ON THE WAY BACK TONIGHT IF YOU'RE LUCKY'.
CUT TO CU CHRIS FOR REACTION SHOT.
CUT TO PAUL AND DAVE HIDING ROUND THE CORNER OF THE BUILDING. WE HEAR THEIR
LAUGHTER.
CUT TO CHRIS AS HE HEARS THE LAUGHTER AND TURNS TOWARDS IT.
CUT TO DAVE AND PAUL, IN HYSTERICS.
CUT TO CHRIS AS HE SEES THEM. HE MOUTHS AN OBVIOUS OBSCENITY WHICH IS DROWNED
OUT BY A CAR HORN. CHRIS JUMPS.
CUT TO MED. SHOT WHICH SHOWS THAT A CAR IS IMMEDIATELY BEHIND CHRIS AND HIS GUI-
TAR IS IN DANGER. CHRIS TURNS AND PICKS UP THE GUITAR.

COMMENTARY Note the number of times the instruction CUT TO is given as the writer in this extract tries to show what is seen by the camera, and therefore by the audience watching the television screen. This should serve to remind you that you must think visually when writing for film or TV. Not all of your script will be dialogue.

ACTIVITY 10

Popular television series or films are often 'novelised' ie adapted as prose fiction.

■ Rewrite the extract from *Calais in the Morning* as a 3rd person prose narrative. This will make you think about when you must let the camera do your descriptive work as opposed to writing the words to describe character, reaction and location.

Writing for films – the screenplay

The technical vocabulary of a screenplay is more extensive than that of the television or radio script and of the types of script considered is probably the most difficult. However, do not let this put you off attempting it.

There are many screenplays published now so it is very easy to obtain examples for study. The example printed below is from the opening to *Star Wars – A New Hope*, the first story in the *Star Wars* trilogy written by George Lucas.

There are minor differences between the layout of the screenplay and the other scripts we have examined. You will notice that capital letters are not used for the descriptive sections of the script but other conventions are the same as those for television such as indicating whether as scene is exterior (EXT) or interior (INT).

TEXT 16

Star Wars – A New Hope

A long time ago in a galaxy far, far away . . .

A vast sea of stars serves as the backdrop for the main title. War drums echo through the heavens as a roll-up slowly crawls into infinity.

It is a period of civil war. Rebel spaceships, striking from a hidden base, have won their first victory against the evil Galactic Empire.

During the battle, Rebel spies managed to steal secret plans to the Empire's ultimate weapon, the Death Star, an armoured space station with enough power to destroy an entire planet.

Pursued by the Empire's sinister agents, Princess Leia races home aboard her starship, custodian of the stolen plans that can save her people and restore freedom to the galaxy.

The awesome yellow planet of Tatooine emerges from a total eclipse, her two moons glowing against the darkness. A tiny silver spacecraft, a Rebel Blockade Runner firing lasers from the back of the ship, races through space. It is pursued by a giant Imperial starship. Hundreds of deadly laserbolts streak from the Imperial Destroyer, causing the main solar fin of the Rebel craft to disintegrate.

INT   REBEL BLOCKADE RUNNER – MAIN PASSAGEWAY

An explosion rocks the ship as two robots, Artoo-Detoo (R2-D2) and See-Threepio (C3-PO), struggle to make their way through the shaking, bouncing passageway. Both robots are old and battered. Artoo is a short, claw-armed tripod. His face is a mass of computer lights surrounding a radar eye. Threepio, on the other hand, is a tall, slender robot of human proportions. He has a gleaming bronze-like metallic surface of an Art Deco design.

Another blast shakes them as they struggle along their way.

THREEPIO: Did you hear that? They've shut down the main reactor. We'll be destroyed for sure. This is madness!

Rebel troopers rush past the robots and take up positions in the main passageway. They aim their weapons towards the door.

THREEPIO: We're doomed!

The little R2 unit makes a series of electronic sounds that only another robot could understand.

THREEPIO: There'll be no escape for the princess this time.

Artoo continues making beeping sounds. Tension mounts as loud metallic latches clank and the screams of heavy equipment are heard moving round the outside hull of the ship.

THREEPIO: What's that?

EXT   SPACECRAFT IN SPACE

The Imperial craft has easily overtaken the Rebel Blockade Runner. The smaller Rebel ship is being drawn into the underside deck of the giant Imperial starship.

INT   REBEL BLOCKADE RUNNER

The nervous Rebel troopers aim their weapons. Suddenly a tremendous blast opens up a hole in the main passageway and a score of fearsome armoured spacesuited stormtroopers make their way into the smoke-filled corridor.

In a few minutes the entire passageway is ablaze with laserfire. The deadly bolts ricochet in wild random patterns creating huge explosions. Stormtroopers scatter and duck behind storage lockers. Laserbolts hit several Rebel soldiers, who scream and stagger through the smoke, holding shattered arms and faces.

THREEPIO: I should have known better than to trust the logic of a half-sized thermocapsulary dehousing assister . . .

Artoo counters with an angry rebuttal as the battle rages around the two hapless robots.

EXT   TATOOINE – DESERT WASTELAND – DAY

A death-white wasteland stretches from horizon to horizon. The tremendous heat of two huge suns settles on a lone figure, Luke Skywalker, a farm boy with heroic aspirations who looks much younger than his eighteen years. His shaggy hair and baggy tunic give him the air of a simple but loveable lad with a prize-winning smile.

A light wind whips at him as he adjusts several valves on a large battered moisture vaporator which sticks out of the desert floor much like an oil pipe with valves. He is aided by a beat-up tread-robot with six claw arms. The little robot appears to be barely functioning and moves with jerky motions. A bright sparkle in the morning sky catches Luke's eye and he instinctively grabs a pair of electrobinoculars from his utility belt. He stands transfixed for a few moments studying the heavens, then dashes towards his dented, crudely repaired landspeeder (an auto-like transport that travels a few feet above the ground on a magnetic field). He motions for the tiny robot to follow him.

LUKE: Hurry up! Come with me! What are you waiting for? Get in gear!

The robot scoots around in a tight circle, stops short, and smoke begins to pour out of every joint. Luke throws his arms up in disgust. Exasperated, the young boy jumps into his landspeeder, leaving the smouldering robot to hum madly.

INT   REBEL BLOCKADE RUNNER – MAIN HALLWAY

The awesome, seven-foot tall Dark Lord of the Sith makes his way into the blinding light of the main passageway. This is Darth Vader, right hand of the Emperor. His face is obscured by his flowing black robes and grotesque breath mask, which stands out next to the fascist white armoured suits of the Imperial stormtroopers.

Everyone instinctively backs away from the imposing warrior and a deathly quiet sweeps through the Rebel troops. Several of the Rebels break and run in a frenzied panic.

INT   REBEL BLOCKADE RUNNER

A woman's hand puts a card into an opening in Artoo's dome. Artoo makes beeping sounds.

ACTIVITY 11

1 Look at the total number of words in this extract. How many are spoken? How many are devoted to what is seen on the screen? The answer is typical of screenplays and should give you an idea of the balance you should aim at in your own screenplay.
2 The main *Star Wars* characters are introduced in this short extract – what is learned of them from these opening sequences from the film?

3 Write a short scene, using the conventions of layout shown in the extract, in which three characters, not necessarily from *Star Wars* are in a life or death situation. This could be a scene from a war, or during a natural disaster such as a cave-in or flood. Remember that most of the script will be devoted to what the audience sees!

3 Argument, Persuasion and Propaganda

In this section we're going to examine language as it is used to influence us. We'll look at its use from persuading us of the correctness of vegetarianism to convincing soldiers in World War II to surrender.

Though they are obviously connected, argument, persuasion and propaganda have differences which set them apart from each other.

Argument aims to provoke discussion while persuasion seeks to end it. The meaning of propaganda, however, has changed over the centuries. It has undergone a process known as 'deterioration'. In the early 17th century the Catholic Church founded a committee to spread Catholicism. This committee was called 'The Propaganda' and so, for its early users, the term had connotations of enlightenment and benevolence.

The word then acquired the more general meaning of spreading opinions and principles. In the 20th century sinister overtones were added when propaganda came to mean a stratagem in war by which false information was deliberately spread in order to influence the outcome of the conflict.

Propaganda now has another, usually pejorative (making something worse), meaning connected to the attempts by pressure groups such as political parties and trades unions to influence public opinion.

One writer defined propaganda as a means for, 'influencing the emotional attitudes of others' and stated that, 'the propagandist is for the creation of certain attitudes ... necessarily against others.'

In essence then, a propagandist attempts to arouse a desire and convince that s/he can satisfy it. To do this an appeal to basic emotions such as love, hate, greed, envy, hope, guilt or any other strong feeling is made in the hope of persuading the reader/listener of the 'rightness' of the propagandist's cause.

The Forensic Oration

Many of the techniques we use today to argue or persuade were used in Ancient Greece. In the Athenian law courts of the 5th century BC a defendant, or his representative, was allowed to deliver a Forensic Oration in the hope of obtaining an acquittal. As the purpose of this oration was to vindicate the accused, the speaker was not limited to a logically structured, objective appeal. Getting off was more important than the truth and if an emotional appeal would succeed where logic failed then so be it!

The Deliberative Oration differs from the Forensic in that its aim was to stimulate argument, 'argument' here meaning a logical, controlled consideration of an issue in the hope of convincing the audience of the reasonableness of the speaker's position; not in the more modern sense of a verbal rough-house.

Although the formula for the forensic oration is usually disparaged today, American trial lawyers often resort to the strategies described in Aristotle's *Rhetoric*. It is not unusual for defence lawyers to cloud issues by bringing in character witnesses, attempting to highlight some supposed flaw in the character of a prosecution witness. It is possible that the lawyer will also appeal to some higher feelings such as religion or patriotism even though these do not constitute 'proof' in the legal sense.

During the trial of the English nanny, Louise Woodward, accused in the USA of murdering a young child in her care, the defence called the Headteachers of her junior and high schools to testify to her good character. It was also suggested that the testimony of a prosecution witness might be in doubt because she had once lied in order to get finance to purchase a car.

The suggestion that a police officer in the case of O. J. Simpson, the American film and sports star accused of the murder of his ex-wife, was driven by racist motives was one of the main planks in his defence.

We have already looked at Marc Antony's funeral oration for Julius Caesar (p 3). On the surface it appears to be the act of a friend, but Antony's real aim is to stir up the Roman populace against the conspirators, who have murdered Caesar. To do this he not only sets out to disprove Brutus' assertion that Caesar was ambitious, but displays the corpse, teases the citizens with Caesar's will, reminds them of Caesar's bravery on their behalf and shows them the stab wounds, naming the conspirator responsible for each one.

The forensic oration consisted of four parts:

1 an analysis of the problem
2 the proposed solution
3 a refutation of the opposing evidence
4 evidence for the defence.

In addition, the speaker might end with a summing up or closing emotional appeal called the 'peroration'.

It is because the forensic oration has a definite aim, ie to gain freedom for the defendant, that it is such an important element in the examination of persuasive techniques.

Text 17 is an extract from *The Apology of Socrates*, which was reported after his death by his student, Plato.

Socrates had been sentenced to death for 'corrupting the youth of Athens'.

He had drawn disapproval down on himself by engaging all and sundry in discussion designed to expose pride and folly and was tried on the charge of impiety (irreligious or blasphemous remarks).

ACTIVITY 12

1 In small groups, discuss the extract and identify where each of the parts of the Forensic Oration is to be found.

2 What are the other persuasive and rhetorical uses of language that Socrates employs?

TEXT 17

Someone will say: And are you not ashamed, Socrates, of a course of life which is likely to bring you to an untimely end? To him I may fairly answer: there you are mistaken: a man who is good for anything ought not to calculate the chance of living or dying; he ought only to consider whether in doing anything he is doing right or wrong – acting the part of a good man or a bad.

Strange indeed would be my conduct, O men of Athens, if I, who when I was ordered by the generals whom you chose to command me at Potidaea and Amphipolis and Delium, remained where they placed me, like any other man, facing death – if now, when as I conceive and imagine, God orders me to fulfil the philosopher's mission of searching into myself and other men, I were to desert my post through fear of death or any other fear; that would indeed be strange, and I might justly be arraigned in court for denying the existence of the gods if I disobeyed the oracle because I was afraid of death, fancying that I was wise when I was not wise.

For the fear of death is indeed a pretence of wisdom, and not real wisdom, being a pretence of knowing the unknown; and no one knows whether death, which men in their fear apprehend to be the greatest evil, might not be the greatest good. Is not this ignorance of a disgraceful sort, the ignorance which is the conceit that a man knows what he does not know? And in this respect only I believe myself to differ from men in general, and may perhaps claim to be wiser than they are; that whereas I know but little of the world below, I do not suppose that I know; but I do know that injustice and disobedience to a better, whether God or man, is evil and dishonourable, and I will never fear or avoid a possible good rather than a certain evil.

And therefore if you let me go now, and are not convinced by Anytus [One of Socrates' accusers], who said that since I had been prosecuted I must be put to death (or if not, that I ought never to have been prosecuted at all), and that if I escape now, your sons will all be utterly ruined by listening to my words – if you say to me, 'Socrates, this time we will not heed Anytus and you shall be let off, but upon one condition, that you are not to inquire and speculate in this way any more, and that if you are caught doing so again you shall die.' If this was the condition on which you let me go; I should reply, Men of Athens, I honour and love you; but I shall obey God rather than you, and while I have life and strength I shall never cease from the practice and teaching of philosophy, exhorting anyone whom I meet and saying to him after my manner: 'You, my friend – a citizen of the great and mighty and wise city of Athens – are you not ashamed of heaping up the greatest amount of money and honour and reputation, and caring so little about wisdom and truth and the greatest improvement of the soul, which you never regard or heed at all?' And if the person with whom I am arguing says, 'Yes, but I do care', then I do not leave him or let him go at once; but I proceed to interrogate and examine and cross examine him, and if I think that he has no virtue in him, but only says he has, I reproach him with undervaluing the greater and overvaluing the less. And I shall repeat the same words to everyone whom I meet, young and old, citizen and alien, but especially to the citizens, inasmuch as they are my brethren. For know that this is the command of God; and I believe that no greater good has ever happened in the state than my service to the God. For I do nothing but go about persuading you all, young and old alike, not to take thought for your persons or your properties, but first and chiefly to care about the greatest improvement of the soul. I tell you that virtue is not given by money, but that from virtue comes money and every other good of man, public as well as private. This is my teaching, and if this is the teaching that corrupts our youth I am a mischievous person. But if anyone says that this is not my teaching, he is speaking an untruth. Wherefore, O men of Athens, I say to you, do as Anytus bids or not as Anytus bids, and either acquit me or not; but whichever you do, understand that I shall never alter my ways, not even if I have to die many times.

Men of Athens, do not interrupt, but hear me; there was an understanding between us that you should hear me to the end; I have something more to say, as which you may be inclined to cry out; but I believe that to hear me will be good for you, and therefore I beg you not to cry out. I would have you know that if you kill such a one as I am, you will injure yourselves more than you will injure me. Nothing will injure me, not Meletus nor yet Anytus – they cannot, for a bad man is not permitted to injure a better than himself. I do not deny that Anytus may, perhaps, kill him, or drive him into exile, or deprive him of civil rights; and he many imagine, and others may imagine, that he is inflicting a great injury upon him; but there I do not agree. For the evil of doing as he is doing – the evil of unjustly taking away the life of another – is greater far.

And now, Athenians, I am not going to argue for my own sake, as you may think, but for yours, that you may not sin against the God by condemning me, who am his gift to you, For if you kill me you will not easily find a successor to me, who, if I may use such a ludicrous figure of speech, am a sort of gadfly given to the state by God; and the state is a great and noble steed who is tardy in his motions owing to his very size, and requires to be stirred into life. I am that gadfly which God has attached to the state, and all day long and in all places am always fastening upon you, arousing and persuading and reproaching you. You will not easily find another like me, and therefore I would advise you to spare me. I dare say that you may feel out of temper (like a person who has suddenly woken from sleep), and you think that you might easily strike me dead as Anytus advises, and then you would sleep on for the remainder of your lives, unless God in his care of you sent you another gadfly. When I say that I am given to you by God, the proof of my mission is this; if I had been like other men, I should not have neglected all my own concerns or patiently seen the neglect of them during all these years, and have been doing yours, coming to you individually like a father or elder brother, exhorting you to regard virtue; such conduct, I say, would be unlike human nature. If I had gained anything, or if my exhortations had been paid, there would have been some sense in my doing so; but now, as you will perceive, not even the impudence of my accusers dares to say that I have ever exacted or sought pay of anyone; of that they have no witness. And I have a sufficient witness to the truth of what I say – my poverty.

Someone may wonder why I go about in private giving advice and busying myself with the concerns of others, but do not venture to come forward in public and advise the state. I will tell you why. You have heard me speak at sundry times and in diverse places of an oracle or sign which comes to me, and is the divinity which Meletus ridicules in the indictment. This sign, which is a kind of voice, first began to come to me when I was a child; it always forbids but never commands me to do anything which I am going to do. This is what deters me from being a politician. And rightly, as I think. For I am certain, O men of Athens, that if I had engaged in politics, I should have perished long ago, and done no good either to you or to myself. And do not be offended at my telling you the truth; for the truth is, that no man who goes to war with you or any other multitude, honestly striving against the many lawless and unrighteous deeds which are done in a state, will save his life; he who will fight for the right, if he would live even for a brief space, must have a private station and not a public one.

COMMENTARY   If we examine the language used by Socrates in this extract we can see many points of interest. Much use is made of the two-part contrast. Examples of this are:

- living or dying
- right or wrong
- acting the part of a good man or of a bad
- fancying that I was wise when I was not wise
- the pretence of wisdom and not real wisdom
- which men in their fear apprehend to be the greatest evil, may not be the greatest good.

Another device he uses is the three-part build up or three-part list. Examples of this are:

- a citizen of the great and mighty and wise city of Athens
- money and honour and reputation
- I proceed to interrogate and examine and cross-examine
- kill him, or drive him into exile or deprive him of civil rights.

He also uses the direct address – 'O men of Athens' and often draws the assembled Athenians into the oration by saying 'you' and 'yourselves'.

There are a number of rhetorical questions – questions to which an answer is not expected.

- Socrates identifies his opposition by name – Anytus and Meletus
- he uses metaphorical language, referring to himself as a gadfly and the state as a slow moving horse which needs goading occasionally
- he attempts a religious justification for his actions.

All these techniques of persuasion and more are still used today and you might use them in your own writing, perhaps without even thinking about them. However, if you did use any of the above and failed to mention it in your commentary, you would have missed an opportunity to show just how in control of language you are.

The Deliberative Oration

Stage One is the introduction to and analysis of the problem. This should be non-partisan and balanced as, if bias is present at this stage, the aim of the argument is defeated before it starts.

Stage Two is the speaker's proposed solution to the problem. In fact, this stage is a moveable one. It might be placed later in the speech, used again in a summary of points made or used as a conclusion.

Stage Three is the refutation of any opposing views but a difference to the forensic oration is that it is possible in a deliberative oration to admit that the other side's ideas might have some merit.

Stage Four concentrates on the speaker's evidence that his position is the one the audience should adopt. In other words, the conclusion.

Both types of oration belong to the tradition of rhetoric – the craft of speaking. Today the word 'rhetoric' has three meanings:

1 the study and practice of communication using eloquent, elegant speech
2 the art of persuasion
3 insincere oratory using artificial and ostentatious expression to convince the gullible.

As the third meaning suggests, rhetoric, like propaganda, has undergone deterioration of meaning over the centuries. Aristotle could never have imagined that some of the skills of public speaking he outlined would be, in the 20th century, used to sell motorcars!

ACTIVITY 13

1 Look again at Marc Antony's funeral oration (p 3) and you will see that Shakespeare used a number of the same linguistic devices as Socrates in his apology. In pairs, analyse the speech and list all the examples of:

a the direct address
b use of contrasts
c repetition of key ideas or phrases.

COMMENTARY Repetition features a great deal in the speech, and repetition is a useful tool in persuasion. However, Marc Antony repeats the phrase about Brutus being 'an honourable man' so often that by the end of the speech we are in no doubt that he means the opposite. The lesson for you when you write your own piece is that repetition is a device to be used with care. It should be a rapier not a broad-sword.

The techniques of persuasion as outlined by Aristotle and other writers who produced guidelines for rhetoric remained at the core of education in medieval Europe as late as the Renaissance. It was during the Renaissance that the emphasis of rhetoric began to shift from speech to writing and today the same tools used by Socrates in Text 17 are used by any individual or group hoping to influence the opinions of others.

The American humorist, P. J. O'Rourke demonstrates in Text 18 that even when a writer adopts a farcical position or writes tongue-in-cheek (something the reader cannot always take for granted with P. J. O'Rourke) the techniques of persuasion are still the same. O'Rourke is a contradictory character who writes from a politically right-wing perspective but who has a background as a rebellious student/hippie which would lead the reader to suspect he is far more liberal than some of his collections of work would suggest. In books such as *Republican Party Reptile*, *Give War a Chance* and *Holidays in Hell*, O'Rourke often assumes a politically incorrect stance. The article below originally appeared in the American magazine *Car and Driver*, the title and implied readership giving some clue as to why he adopts the tone he does.

ACTIVITY 14

In pairs, read O'Rourke's piece carefully.

1 Analyse the persuasive techniques he uses.

2 Are any of them present in *The Apology of Socrates*?

TEXT 18
A COOL AND LOGICAL ANALYSIS OF THE BICYCLE MENACE

(And an examination of the actions necessary to license, regulate, or abolish entirely this dreadful peril on our roads)

Our nation is afflicted with a plague of bicycles. Everywhere the public right of way is glutted with whirring, unbalanced contraptions of rubber, wire and cheap steel pipe. Riders of these flimsy appliances pay no heed to stop signs or red lights. They dart from between parked cars, dash along double yellow lines, and whiz through crosswalks right over the toes of law-abiding citizens like me.

In the cities, every lamppost, tree and street sign is disfigured by a bicycle slathered in chains and locks. And elevators must be shared with the cycling faddist so attached to his 'moron's bathchair' that he has to take it with him everywhere he goes.

In the country, one cannot drive around a curve or over the crest of a hill without encountering a gaggle of huffing bicyclers spread across the road in suicidal phalanx.

Even the wilderness is not safe from infestation, as there is now such a thing as an off-road bicycle and a horrible sport called 'bicycle cross'.

The ungainly geometry and primitive mechanicals are an offence to the eye. The grimy and perspiring riders of the bicycle are an offence to the nose. And the very existence of the bicycle is an offence to reason and wisdom.

PRINCIPAL ARGUMENTS WHICH MAY BE MARSHALLED AGAINST BICYCLES

BICYCLES ARE CHILDISH

Bicycles have their proper place, and that place is under small boys delivering evening papers. Insofar as children are too short to see over the dashboards of cars and too small to keep motorcycles upright at intersections, bicycles are suitable vehicles for them. But what are we to make of an adult in a suit pedalling his way to work? Are we to assume he still delivers newspapers for a living? If not, do we want a doctor, lawyer or business executive who plays with toys? St Paul, in his First Epistle to the Corinthians, 13:11, said, 'When I became a man, I put away childish things.' He did not say, 'When I became a man I put away childish things and got more elaborate and expensive childish things from France and Japan.' Considering the image projected, bicycling commuters might as well propel themselves to the office with one knee in a red Radio Flyer wagon.

BICYCLES ARE UNDIGNIFIED

A certain childishness is, no doubt, excusable. But going about in public with one's head between one's knees and one's rump protruding in the air is nobody's idea of acceptable behaviour.

It is impossible for an adult to sit on a bicycle without looking the fool. There is a type of woman, in particular, who should never assume the bicycling posture. This is the woman of ample proportions. Standing on her own feet she is a figure to admire – classical in her beauty and a symbol, throughout history, of sensuality, maternal virtue, and plenty. Mounted on a bicycle, she is a laughing stock.

BICYCLES ARE UNSAFE

Bicycles are top-heavy, have poor brakes, and provide no protection to their riders. Bicycles are also made up of many hard and sharp components which, in collision, can do grave damage to people and the paint finish on automobiles. Bicycles are dangerous things.

Of course, there's nothing wrong, per se, with dangerous things. Speedboats, racecars, fine shotguns, whiskey and love are all very dangerous. Bicycles, however, are dangerous without being any fun. You can't shoot pheasants with a bicycle or water-ski behind it or go 150 miles an hour or even mix it with soda and ice. And the idea of getting romantic on top of a bicycle is alarming. All you can do with one of these ten-speed sink traps is grow tired and sore and fall off it.

Being dangerous without being fun puts bicycles in a category with open-heart surgery, the war in Vietnam, the South Bronx and divorce. Sensible people do all that they can to avoid such things as these.

BICYCLES ARE UN-AMERICAN

We are a nation that worships speed and power. And for good reason. Without power we would still be part of England and everybody would be out of work. And if it weren't for speed, it would take us months to fly to LA, get involved in the movie business, and become rich and famous.

Bicycles are too slow and impuissant for a country like ours. They belong in Czechoslovakia.

I DON'T LIKE THE KIND OF PEOPLE WHO RIDE BICYCLES

At least, I think I don't. I don't actually know anyone who rides a bicycle. But the people I see on bicycles look like organic-gardening zealots who advocate federal regulation of bedtime and want American foreign policy dictated by UNICEF. These people should be confined.

I apologise if I have the wrong impression. It may be that bicycle riders are members of the New York Stock Exchange, Methodist Bishops, retired Marine Corps instructors and other solid citizens. However, the fact that they cycle round in broad daylight making themselves look like idiots indicates that they're crazy anyway and should be confined just the same.

BICYCLES ARE UNFAIR

Bicycles use the same roads as cars and trucks yet they pay no gasoline tax, carry no licence plates, are not required to have insurance, and are not subject to other regulations. Furthermore, bicyclists do not have to take driver's examinations, have eye tests when they're over sixty-five, carry registration papers with them or submit to breathalyser tests under threat of law. And they never get caught in radar traps. The fact that bicycles are ridden by the very people who most favour government interference in life makes the bicycle's special status not only unfair but an outright incitement to riot.

Equality before the law is the cornerstone of democracy. Bicycles should be made to carry twenty-gallon tanks full of gasoline. They should be equipped with twelve-volt batteries and a full complement of tail-lights, head-lamps and turn-signals. They should have seat belts, air bags, and safety glass windows too. And every bicycle rider should be inspected once a year for hazardous defects and be made to wear a number plate hanging round his neck and another on the seat of his pants.

BICYCLES ARE GOOD EXERCISE

And so is swinging through the trees on your tail. Mankind has invested more than four million years of evolution in the attempt to avoid physical exercise. Now a group of backward-thinking atavists mounted on foot-powered hula-hoops would have us pumping our legs, gritting our teeth, and searing our lungs as though we were being chased across the Pleistocene savannah by sabre-toothed tigers. Think of all the hopes, the dreams, the effort, the brilliance, the pure force of will, that over the eons has gone into the creation of the Cadillac Coupe de Ville. Bicycle riders would have us throw all this on the ash heap of history.

WHAT MUST BE DONE ABOUT THE BICYCLE THREAT?

Fortunately, nothing. Frustrated truck drivers and irate cabbies make a point of running bicycles off the road. Terrified old ladies jam umbrella ferrules into wheel spokes as bicycles rush by them on sidewalks. And all of us have occasion to back over bicycles that are haplessly parked.

Bicycles are quiet and slight, difficult for normal motorised humans to see and hear. People pull out in front of bicycles, open car doors in their path, and drive through intersections filled with the things.

The insubstantial bicycle and its unshielded rider are defenceless against these actions. It's a simple matter of natural selection. The bicycle will be extinct within the decade. And what a relief that will be.

COMMENTARY   Let's look at the similarities between O'Rourke's article and the apology of Socrates. O'Rourke analyses 'the problem'. He offers much 'evidence' in favour of his position and disparages the opposition. He then suggests a solution to the problem, or rather, states that a solution is already working.

O'Rourke uses a number of other 'tricks' of writing to persuade. These include:

1 appeals to patriotism
2 biblical references
3 use of an academic vocabulary to establish an air of authority – *impuissant, atavists, phalanx*, use of the Latin phrase *'per se'*
4 appeal to a higher concept ie democracy
5 use of a vocabulary chosen to foreground his low opinion of bicycles and their riders, for example, a *plague of bicycles, infestation, zealots, backward-thinking atavists*
6 the 'three-part build-up' as in:
   > *'The ungainly geometry and primitive mechanicals are an offence to the eye.'*
   > *'The grimy and perspiring riders of the bicycle are an offence to the nose.'*
   > *'And the very existence of the bicycle is an offence to reason and wisdom.'*

These sentences also demonstrate how O'Rourke uses parallel sentence construction to build to his point.

Remember that the audience for which this is written is comprised of car owners and probably, as they buy a magazine entitled *Car and Driver*, car owners who are not merely concerned that their car gets them from A to B.

He sets out his stall in his opening paragraph using the emotive words: *afflicted*, *plague* and *infestation*. An *affliction* being something which causes distress, a *plague* is a lethal epidemic and an *infestation* is usually to do with being overrun with parasites. He maintains this hyperbole (extravagant exaggeration) throughout the article – for example, 'disfigure the landscape'.

Infestation, plague, affliction and disfigure all belong to that group of words to do with illness and disease. We call this using words from the same semantic field. If you want to use a 'trick' like this in your own writing, for example, to foreground the idea of 'waste' in a piece on recycling, use a thesaurus. Under 'waste', you would find: desolation, devour, eliminate, exhaust, exterminate, extravagance, fritter, profligacy and many other words from the same semantic field you might usefully employ.

His low opinion of the bicycle is also foregrounded by a series of derogatory descriptions such as: *cheap steel pipe*, *flimsy appliances*, *moron's bathchair*, *primitive mechanicals*, and *foot-powered hula-hoops*.

The people who ride bicycles are treated similarly being described as *faddists* (people who follow a trivial craze), a *gaggle* (usually applied to geese) and *zealots* (fanatics). He extends this idea to suggest that cyclists are also *childish*, a *laughing stock* or *atavists* (primitive throwbacks). On the other hand, people like O'Rourke are law-abiding citizens, or so irritated by cyclists that they become frustrated and irate. Motorists are also normal, suggesting that people who do not drive are abnormal.

It is suggested that to prefer a bicycle to the automobile is somehow un-American. The appeal to patriotism is a very strong one in persuasion. He continues this appeal with his reference to Our Nation and takes some swipes at England, France and Japan.

A device variously referred to as the three-part build-up, three part lists and rule of three is also employed. This is often combined with parallel sentence construction (using sentences following the same syntactical pattern). We see this in the openings to the 2nd, 3rd and 4th paragraphs:

> para 2 – In the cities . . .
> para 3 – In the country . . .
> para 4 – Even in the wilderness . . .

These elements are combined to build to the climax of the 5th paragraph:

The ungainly geometry and primitive mechanicals of the bicycle are an offence to the eye. The grimy and perspiring riders of the bicycle are offence to the nose. And the very existence of the bicycle is an offence to reason and wisdom.

In section 3 O'Rourke uses the device once again in:

Bicycles are top-heavy, have poor brakes and provide no protection to their riders.

In the concluding paragraph we find:

People pull out in front of bicycles, open car doors in their path, and drive through intersections filled with the things.

It is always a good idea to suggest that the weight of authority is behind you when attempting to persuade. O'Rourke quotes St. Paul in his First Epistle to the Corinthians turning it to his own ends. Shakespeare acknowledged the power of scriptural references when he had Richard III say:

But then I sigh, and, with a piece of Scripture,
Tell them that God bids us do good for evil;
And thus I clothe my naked villainy
With odd old ends stolen forth of Holy Writ.
And seem a saint, when most I play the devil.

Richard III Act 1, Scene 3, lines 333–338

O'Rourke also uses an academic vocabulary to establish an air of intellectuality. Examples of this are: *phalanx*, a Greek word meaning a formation of heavily armed infantry, the Latin phrase *per se* meaning in itself, and *impuissant*, from the French and meaning powerless.

And just as Socrates offered a possible solution to the problem for the Athenian assembly, O'Rourke suggests the answer to the bicycle menace, or rather states that a solution is already working. This is that scientific principle, ie natural selection, will solve the problem without any help from motorists.

Propaganda

During World War II both the Allied and the Axis powers made great use of propaganda to try to influence the conflict. One tactic employed was the dropping of leaflets on enemy lines in attempts to persuade the adversary to retreat, consider his fate or generally to undermine his morale.

Text 19 is taken from a leaflet dropped on the Allied troops by the German airforce as the Americans advanced through Italy in the later stages of the war. On one side of the leaflet is a photograph of a scantily-clad young woman wearing an American army helmet at a jaunty angle. In the foreground is an illustration showing a soldier who has just been shot falling across a barbed-wire fence. The leaflet was one of a series of six and, as you will read, it was suggested that the allied soldiers might like to collect them all.

ACTIVITY 15

In small groups read *Winter Weather Ahead*.

1 Identify the emotions the Nazi propagandist has tried to play on.

2 What other techniques has the writer used to try to convince the Allied soldiers that their position was hopeless?

TEXT 19

WINTER WEATHER AHEAD!

The days are shortening and you are still here. " Beautiful Italy " has changed. That bit of sun during the day cannot warm you any more after you have been lying for days and days in your foxholes perhaps knee deep in water.

True enough Jerry is giving up a bit of ground here aud there. Perhaps he will give up a few miles again some day, but only after he has exacted the highest possible toll of blood from your infantrymen.

WHAT WOULD YOU BE FACING THEN ?

The mighty swift-flowing Po river with its deep ice-cold water and a merciless fire sweeping across from the other side.

WHAT WOULD YOU SEE after you had perhaps managed to build a bridge over the river on the bodies of your comrades? Just new fort-ifications, a maze of barbed wire entanglements, thousands of pill-boxes, earthworks, concrete and steel for miles! All the long weary way to the Alps, the highest and most difficult mountain barrier in Europe, with ridges of tenthousand feet and an eternal winter.

EACH LINE MUST BE STORMED AND THOUSANDS OF AMERI-CANS WILL HAVE TO GIVE THEIR LIVES !

AND AT HOME ?

They know very little about your sufferings out here in Italy. The ignor-ance on the subject has never been greater than now. The home-front warriors, especially the Hebrews, are rolling in cash and praying that this war may go on for ever. They are launching " reconnaissance parties " too, but into the bedrooms of lonely women. Their ammunit-ion is a fat roll of bills and their war-cry is : MORE DOLLARS AND GIRLS. They get them !

HAS IT NEVER OCCURED TO YOU HOW SENSELESS all this is, and that nobody will give you any thanks afterwards ?

You can do nothing about it ?   *Oh yes, you can !*

You can think of your own nearest and dearest at home. You know in your hearts that, whatever their sentiments about dead heroes may be, the very best news any of them can receive is that you are wait-ing for the end of the war safe and sound in a decent camp.

Give them a Happy Christmas !

Georgia series comprising 6 pictures. Have you got the others?

COMMENTARY In the text of this leaflet we can see how the Nazi propagandist has tried to arouse the feelings of envy, fear, hope and love:

- envy of 'the Home Front Warriors' who are allegedly having a good time back at home
- fear of dying in the advance across Italy
- hope of survival, if necessary by surrendering to see out the war in a prisoner of war camp
- love of family – mention of 'nearest and dearest' and mention of a 'Happy Christmas'
- there is also the attempt to make the Nazis appear less belligerent and threatening by use of the more personal nickname 'Jerry'.

The writer of the leaflet also attempts to deflect the hostility of the advancing forces onto 'The Hebrews'. Such labelling is known as 'pinpointing the enemy' and focuses the attention of the reader on the supposed enemy. During the 1982 Falklands War some of the British tabloids used the same tactic in headlines such as 'Argy Bargy' and referring to the Argentine soldiers as 'Argies'.

A group of words which would be extremely familiar to the soldier-readers shows that the writer had his audience very clearly in focus. These words include: *foxholes, pillboxes, reconnaissance* and many others.

Text 20 is another leaflet which was dropped by the Nazis, this time on British troops advancing towards Berlin. The tone of this leaflet is slightly different to the one dropped in Italy. There are, however, a number of linguistic devices we have already encountered.

ACTIVITY 16

On your own, write an analysis of the propaganda techniques used by the German writer of Text 20 to influence British soldiers.

TEXT 20

He also had been told

that the Germans are a horde of Huns and barbarians, posing as supermen and with only one idea, to bring all Europe under their tyranny of terror.

He also had been told

that it was the sacred duty of all liberty-loving men to free Europe from the bestial cruelty of these Nazis.

He also had been told

that in fighting against these Huns it was necessary to hold out to the last, as the Germans illtreat and even kill their prisoners.

The day came when he was taken prisoner.

The „Hun" who had captured him pulled out his first-aid kit, bandaged his wounded hand and gave him a cigarette.
The „Hun" who brought him to the dressing station gave him a drink from his own flask and saw to it that hat he came under the doctor's care at once.
The „Hun" doctor who skilfully and gently extracted the splinter from his hand, gave him another cigarette and sent him off with a friendly pat on the back.
The „Hun" who brought him to the prisoners' camp knew a little English and told him and some of his pals all about his home and his family.

Then he understood

that all these German soldiers were neither Huns nor wild beasts nor did they pose as supermen. They were boys like his friends Bill, Fred and George, boys with the same joys and sorrows. They had the same claims on life as the English soldiers and, like them, they were also fed up with war.

And so everything was quite different

from what his newspapers and wireless, full of hate-propaganda, had been dinning into his ears. He had been the victim of a swindle, for he knew well enough now from all the German soldiers he had met and learned to know, that they were incapable of committing the atrocities recounted daily by his papers. They wanted to live in peace and attend to their work, and for this it was necessary that the world should allow them the same rights as any other nation. They were fighting for these rights and would not cease fighting until they obtained them. But nothing was further from their thoughts than to wish to dominate Europe. On the contrary, on their Eastern Front they were fighting the battle of this very Europe against the Asiatic hordes of the steppes beyond the Urals and the Caucasus, who, stirred up by Bolshevism, had attacked Europe with murder, violence and robbery. They would not be satisfied with the conquest of Germany alone, their goal was the revolutionising of the whole world. And while the Germans were fighting desperately against this onslaught, they were defending not only their own lives but were fighting for Europe and also for England, for him, Bill, Fred, George, and for everyting that made life worth living.

And so he began to reflect!

If everything that the anti-German hate-propaganda was saying was untrue, if the truth was something quite different, then there must be someone with an interest in this senseless slaughter among the nations of Europe. There must be someone who profits by all the suffering and misery of war.
Who is it?

This is a question worth thinking over.

COMMENTARY Some of the linguistic devices used by the writer include parallel sentence construction and three part lists. The enemy is pinpointed when the writer refers to the Asiatic Hordes. We can also see an example of labelling as a method of making things appear worse than they are. Bolshevism is, in the context of the leaflet, not an identification of an early 20th century Russian political party but is used because the word has connotations of cruelty, barbarity and lack of discipline. Our contemporary slang 'Bolshie', meaning uncooperative and lacking discipline, comes from this root.

What is also interesting in the language of this leaflet is that the writer substitutes 'Hun' for German. The original Huns were a warlike race who, under their most famous leader Attila, invaded and ravaged Europe in the 5th century AD. They had a reputation for cruelty and the destruction of art. The term was first applied to the Germans in the war of 1914–18. It is strange that a German propagandist would use this substitution but we are shown that doubt is being cast on the meaning by the fact that each time it is used in quotation marks.

Whether Text 21 is information, persuasion or propaganda is a matter for debate. The leaflet *Space Sheep & Astro Pig* is one of a series of leaflets produced by The Vegetarian Society. It is included because it is unusual to see this type of writing aimed at a young audience. The writers match their text to their audience very skilfully in a number of ways. The leaflet was handed to children as they came out of their junior school.

ACTIVITY 17

Read *Space Sheep and Astro Pig talk about Factory Farming*. Discuss, in pairs, whether this attempt to persuade a young audience differs from the pieces aimed at a mature audience? Are any of the techniques the same?

TEXT 21

Space Sheep & Astro Pig

TALK ABOUT

FACTORY FARMING

Some people may tell you that all farm animals lead a happy life in nice open fields, but this is not true.
Most of the animals I have seen are kept in cruel and horrible places called FACTORY FARMS.

Nearly all the hens are kept in tiny cages where they cannot even turn around or stretch their wings.
When they stop laying enough eggs for the farmer, he kills them.
They are then made into food like chicken soup or chicken pies.

If you want to help stop this cruelty, only eat FREE-RANGE eggs. These eggs are laid by hens that are not kept locked up in cages.
Free-range hens lead a more natural and free life.

I feel very sad and upset to tell you how my friends are treated.
The mummy pig, called a sow, is kept on a cold hard floor, where she has to give birth to her piglets.

She can hardly move as she is enclosed by metal bars, which stop her from reaching her babies properly. Her piglets are taken away from her too early, at only two weeks old.
Young and frightened, they are squashed into small pens where they are fattened.
They are killed before they reach six months old, for bacon, pork and ham.

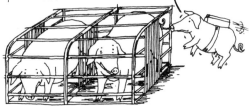

These are only two types of animal that are mistreated in factory farms. We have seen ducks and rabbits locked in tiny cages, and baby calves and their mums (cows) and dads (bulls) crammed into pens where they never see a field in their life.

Many of these animals die in their cages, as they catch diseases and are very unhappy.

Bye!
And don't forget the coupon!

If you want to do something to help these animals, become a vegetarian.
Vegetarians are people who do not eat animals. Thousands of children are already vegetarians, why not join them?

If you need any help or information please write to the address printed on the coupon on the back page of this leaflet.
Or how about joining the Vegetarian Society? The under-12's have their own club, called The Green Gang. Members receive free leaflets, badges, stickers, magazines and other things too!
Don't delay, post the coupon today!

- -
Tick boxes required.

☐ Please send me free information about Vegetarianism.

☐ Please send me ____ more of these leaflets. (Please say how many you want.)

☐ I would like to become a junior member of the Vegetarian Society, and enclose £4.00 I am under 18.

☐ I enclose a donation of £____.

Total amount enclosed £____. (Cheques/ p.o's payable to The Vegetarian Society.)
Date:_____

Name:_____ Date of Birth:_____

Address:_____

Postcode:_____

100% Recycled Paper

The writers have chosen to use anthropomorphism – the attribution of human motives and feelings to non-humans such as animals – as a means of appealing to their audience. Space Sheep and Astro Pig talk about factory farming directly to the children using terms which they would be familiar with. We have a 'mummy pig' and 'baby calves' and 'mums and dads' – a vocabulary of family which is central to youngsters.

It is also in the first person as though the cartoon characters are appealing directly to the audience, making the text quite personal. The vocabulary is accessible and the readability level quite low. There is also the appeal of the illustrations – most of the intended audience would be used to text broken up by illustration. It is probably true that the sheep and pig were given their names because of the current popularity of science fiction related television programmes, films and comics amongst young children. For instance, notice that Space Sheep and Astro Pig have 'jet-packs'.

There is another tactic used here which we have not seen yet though it is a common tool of the propagandist. It is called the 'bandwagon approach'. This is when it is suggested that if you don't agree with an idea or use a product you are somehow out of step. Advertisers often use this technique, for example, '9 out of 10 owners said their cats preferred . . .'. Here the readers are told, 'Thousands of children are already vegetarians'.

There are also uses of language similar to those in the texts already examined. There is much word pairing as in: *cruel and horrible, natural and free, sad and upset, young and frightened.* The adjectives used to premodify the nouns are part of a basic vocabulary familiar to most young readers. We find: *happy life, nice open fields, tiny cages* and *cold, hard floor.*

Lastly, there are a number of things mentioned which are carefully gauged to appeal to youngsters. These are the club for Green Gang members which entitles subscribers to receive leaflets, badges and stickers. The typeface is an imitation of the handwriting style of a young writer.

Political Persuasion

Let's look at an example of modern political oratory. The following is an extract from a speech made by Labour Prime Minister Tony Blair to the 1997 Party Conference. You can make an interesting comparison with the Tory Leader, William Hague's speech to his 1997 Conference. This is featured in *Language and Style*, another book in this series.

TEXT 22

After 18 long years of Opposition, of frustration and despair, I am proud, privileged, to stand before you as the new Labour Prime Minister of our country.

I believe in Britain. I believe in the British people. One cross on the ballot paper. One nation was reborn.

Today I want to set an ambitious course for this country. To be nothing less than the model 21st century nation, a beacon to the world. It means drawing deep into the richness of the British character. Creative. Compassionate. Outward-looking.

Old British values with a new British confidence. We can never be the biggest. We may never again be the mightiest. But we can be the best. The best place to live. The best place to bring up children, the best place to lead a fulfilled life, the best place to grow old.

14 years ago our Party was written off as history. This year we made it. Let our first thanks be to the British people. You kept faith with us. And we will keep faith with you.

Thank you to the Party organisation, the volunteers, the professionals who fashioned the finest political fighting machine anywhere in the world.

And thanks to those that led before me.

To Neil Kinnock*: the mantle of Prime Minister was never his. But I know that without him, it would never have been mine.

To John Smith*: who left us a fine legacy, and to whom we can now leave a fitting monument – a Scottish Parliament in the city where he lived, serving the country he loved and the people who loved him.

To Jim Callaghan*: who was attending Labour Party Conferences before I was born; and by the look of him, will be attending long after I've gone.

My own debt of honour to Michael Foot*: you led this Party when, frankly, it was incapable of being led and without ever losing a shred of your dignity or your integrity. Thank you.

I should also like to say a final word of thanks to the Tory Party. Let's be honest, we'd never have done so well without them.

So thanks to Michael Howard*, to John Redwood*, Peter Lilley*, Brian Mawhinney*. Sorry – 'Sir' Brian Mawhinney – knighted for services to the Conservative Party. John Prescott wanted to give him a peerage – for services to the Labour Party.

As for Government, well, it beats the hell out of Opposition. They really do say 'Yes, Prime Minister'. You have to learn a whole new language. They're not in the habit of calling anything a good idea, which given the last 18 years is hardly surprising.

[*Here 3 paragraphs on the Civil Service are omitted*]

It's not the titles and the cars and the trappings that make government worthwhile. It's letters like this from 11 year old Emma O'Brien from Ellesmere Port.

'Summer School was a good idea. I have started to read more books. I have learned more spellings. We've had fun. All of us have made new friends. I think you and parliament have done the right thing. I have got a better education.'

Or this one from Mrs Patricia Lewis, of South London.

'Each afternoon I collected him from school. By the fourth day the change was showing in Stephen. His enthusiasm grew, confidence gained, his ability to read, write, spell, speak and question politely, was amazing.'

That is why we are here. That is what made winning worth the fight. Ours was not a victory of politicians but of people. The people took their trust, and gave it to us. I want them to say, this week as they watch us here in Brighton: we did the right thing. I want the British people to be as proud of having elected us as we are to serve them.

* Neil Kinnock, John Smith, Jim Callaghan, Michael Foot – Leaders of the Labour Party before Tony Blair.

* Michael Howard, Peter Lilley, John Redwood, Sir Brian Mawhinney – prominent Conservative politicians.

ACTIVITY 18

1 In pairs read the extract from the Prime Minister's speech and identify the techniques of persuasion used – you will find many features we have identified in previous texts in this chapter.

2 On your own, write a speech using many of the techniques you have examined in this chapter in which you attempt to persuade an audience to adopt your point of view or position on a subject about which you feel very strongly.

4 Information, Advice and Exposition

As with other types of writing, it is probably easier when writing to inform, advise or explain if you have some degree of experience or expertise to draw on. Your aim, as a writer, should be to provide clear information and advice. Or as one student put it, 'The writer should want to help the reader in some way'.

If you take a look around any tourist office, doctor's surgery, DIY store or fast-food restaurant you'll see just how much of this type of writing is produced. For instance, a group of students recently visited their city centre and collected a large amount of material on a wide range of subjects from very different organisations. A random selection of titles from the ones they collected illustrates this variety:

- *The Food Standards Agency – A Force for Change* published by HM Government.
- *Fire Safety in the Home – Protect Your Home from Fire* published by The Home Office Directorate.
- *Pet-Lover's Re-homing Programme* published by RSPCA/Tesco.
- *So You Think You Can Handle it?* (Anti-Drinking & Driving Pamphlet) published by Department of the Environment.
- *Help the Aged Millennium Awards* published by Help the Aged.
- *Towards a Better World* published by Chemical Industries Association.
- *Merseytide – Turning the Estuary Management Plan's Vision into Reality* published by Mersey Strategy Steering Group.

Though these are very different subjects and have very different audiences, many of the presentational devices and language structures used are similar in all the publications. They all use:

- illustrations – either photographs or line drawings
- different sizes and types of font
- areas of white space to avoid daunting blocks of print.

And many use:

- graphs
- diagrams
- bullet points.

In fact, success with this type of writing is as easy as ABC. It isn't that simple, of course, ABC is a mnemonic which stands for Accuracy, Brevity and Clarity.

- **accuracy** in terms of the information and advice given and of the written expression
- **brevity** in that extraneous information, or waffle, is detrimental to the successful communication of ideas
- **clarity** so that points are made in a structured and coherent manner.

You should also remember that a lively and imaginative style – as long as this doesn't compromise the accuracy, brevity and clarity – is more likely to be a success than one which is flat and dull.

Remember, the most satisfying writing is often that which arises out of a genuine personal experience of, or involvement in, the subject.

Popular topics for A-Level English Language students often include 'How to …' Guides. For instance, 'How to play table tennis' would fit into the categories we're exploring here but as there are many published books of this sort, a subject such as this can make it difficult for you to be original. If, however, a writer who is a table tennis player puts a personal spin on the subject by writing on 'How to prepare for a Tournament' then her writing is much more likely to be lively and original.

Often you can write successfully about your experience of part-time employment. You might even find that writing which outlines the pleasures and pitfalls of this type of employment produced as a guide for prospective employees may be adopted by the employers as training material.

Text 23 (pages 46–48) is an extract from an extremely successful guide entitled, *So You Want To Work at a Garden Centre*, together with part of the writer's commentary (below). The guide had the added bonus of amusing even those readers who, strictly speaking, were not members of the target audience.

Writer's Commentary

The idea for this informative text came as a consequence of my own experiences of working at a garden centre over the busy summer period, therefore the second person address was used for an added personal touch. The main technique used is humour, with the sub-divisions of the humour being: the imitation of a biblical style, punning (eg 'growth of experience'), garden imagery, sarcasm and the use of jargon, including 'in jokes'.

The final draft contains more cartoons to help bring certain areas across visually and also to add interest by splitting up long sections of text. I decided to split the written text up into different sections as this is a common feature in the organisation of informative booklets. Each section contains different information. I thought this would be an advantageous way of keeping the reader's attention.

In the first section the background history of the garden centre is given. This section contains the biblical humour with references to Adam and Eve and Moses and the Ten Commandments. These are relevant because of the relationship of Adam and Eve to the Garden of Eden.

'More Days & Questions' used a cartoon to illustrate how ludicrously unanswerable many of the questions I got asked were and by using humour in the answers, ie 'Pretend you know the answer … hoping they'll get lost and won't find you to annoy you again', I hoped to show that there was no right way of doing things. I also wrote some ridiculous questions to which the answer was obvious or plain stupid, eg 'Are those red flowers red or white?'

TEXT 23

So you want to work at a garden centre?
PART 1

"...And God Created The Garden Centre?"

It was probably inevitable from the very dawn of civilization that garden centres would be invented. Just think how handy it would have been for Adam and Eve to nip round to the local Jurassic Plant Emporium for a new giant fern or fig tree.

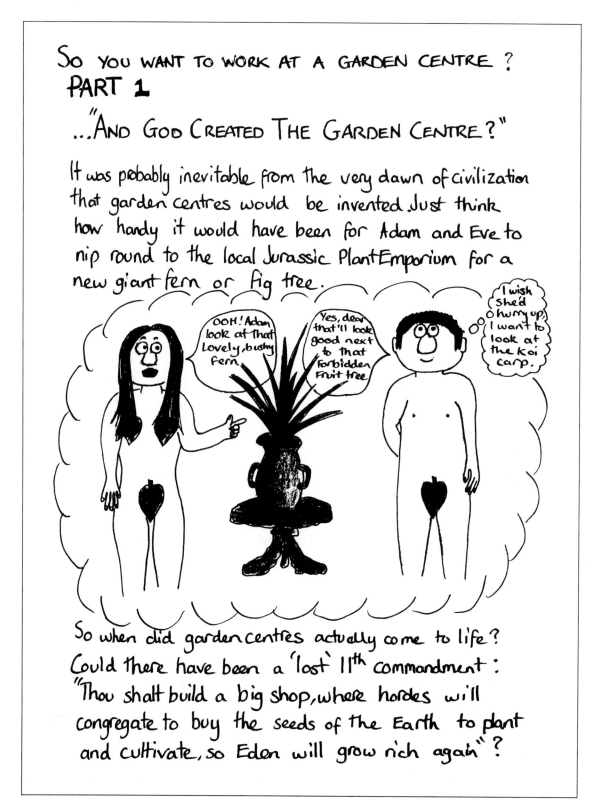

So when did garden centres actually come to life? Could there have been a 'lost' 11th commandment: "Thou shalt build a big shop, where hordes will congregate to buy the seeds of the Earth to plant and cultivate, so Eden will grow rich again"?

PART 4: MORE DAYS, AND QUESTIONS

By the third weekend, you will be proficient at box-making and trolley-wallying and so you will be having urges for something (anything!) more stimulating for your brain. In a flash the stimulation arrives. Whilst just minding your own business restocking Yellow African Marigolds, you receive your first customer enquiry:-

Excuse me could you tell me if you have the variety Calluna Vulgaris Primeria?

Hmmm! A multiple choice answer question, with four choices: (a) (b) (c) or (d)? let me see!:

(a) Pretend you know where it is and just send the customer to the far reaches of the garden centre, hoping they get lost and won't find you to annoy you again:
"Yes, it's just over there, past the sheddius wooduss, right at the carboniferous barbecucius, past the Embothrium Coccineum lanceolatum and then it's opposite the Schizostylis. Is that clear enough?"
b) Pretend not to hear the enquiry hoping they think you are a customer and walk away.

c) Point them to another worker (say, he is a
  specialist in Calluna varieties) then grin cunningly
  as you observe the worker's puzzled face
d) Actually know the answer and smile intensely
  as the customer locates the plant and buys it.*
*This is an extreme rarity, and may never be
  experienced, such questions that are answerable
  are :-
    i) "Could you tell me where the toilets are?"
    ii) "Is this the car-park?"
    iii "Do you know where the trollies are?"
    iv) "Do you know how to make boxes?"
    v) "Are those red flowers red or white?"

Of course, you may not have found the extracts funny. If you set out to amuse you must recognise that comedy is idiosyncratic and that you will inevitably fail to tickle the sense of humour of some of your readers.

ACTIVITY 19

Text 24 (pages 50–51) was also written from personal experience and aimed at a very small target audience, in this case sixth form students at the writer's school who might in future represent the school's public speaking team.

Read *A Guide to Public Speaking* and, in pairs, answer the questions which follow.

1 What are the advantages of choosing this format for the piece?
2 What in the text shows that the guide is aimed at a very specific audience?

3 What in the text would not be understood by those outside the intended audience?
4 What is gained by having cartoons in the leaflet?
5 Is the language of the guide formal, informal or a blend of the two?

The candidate's own commentary, in which these questions are answered, is given at the end of this chapter.

ACTIVITY 20

Produce a brochure, leaflet, or article on your hobby or leisure interests. Think about:

a Audience – who are you writing for? Your peer group, complete beginners, experienced hobbyists?
b Format – do you want to produce an

information sheet as might be found in your local library, a newspaper article for a general audience or a newsletter?
c Tone – is your piece going to be light and humorous or serious and fact-packed?

Do it their way

Another way of approaching this category of informative writing is to imitate some of the features found in publications such as the *Radio Times*, *The Times*, *GQ* and others.

The *Radio Times* carries a feature entitled 'My Kind of Day'. In this feature a celebrity is interviewed and their answers turned into a first person account of a typical day in their lives. The interviewer has asked questions which invite the subject to reveal something of their background, current way of life and attitude to their job.

ACTIVITY 21

Read the 'My Kind of Day' column. What questions do you think the interviewer asked to elicit the information revealed in the article?

TEXT 24 – A Guide to Public Speaking

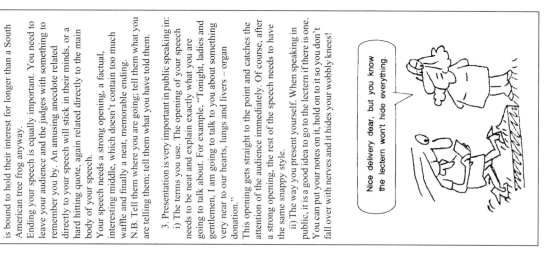

Page 1 (cover)

A GUIDE TO PUBLIC SPEAKING

> Um..... Good evening Ladies and Gentlemen. Errr....

Public Speaking is an important skill, which is useful. Some business opportunities are one chance only, and you want to give them your best shot. By learning through public speaking competitions, you can bring some polish to the performances that really matter!

Page 2

A Guide to Public Speaking

Welcome to the Calder High public speaking team! Now that you are a member of Mrs. Todd's Gals (whether you are female or otherwise!) I'm sure that you are aware of our previous successes at the Associations of Speakers Clubs Youth Competition, the Business and Professional Women's (B.P.W.) and the Hammond Suddard West Yorkshire Schools Debating Competition. So as not to let the side down, here's a leaflet to help you prepare yourself for the ordeal which awaits you! (it's not really that bad!)

Public speaking can be a hair raising experience. With this comprehensive guide, I hope that a lot of nerves can be calmed and a lot of speeches can be improved. By preparing your speech correctly and following the rules, there is no reason for any one to turn to jelly behind the lectern!

1. Decide on your audience.

If you are speaking in a competition, such as the B.P.W., your audience is likely to be other competitors and their supporters, and the elderly ladies who always support the B.P.W. The audience should not affect your choice of subject, although politics and sex are not recommended topics.

Your audience should affect what you choose to say. For example, if you are giving an informal speech in a classroom situation, you aren't going to be using the formal vocabulary which you might use to prospective parents at a parents evening or in a competition. By the same token, in a House of Commons debate, when proposing your motion you are not going to begin in the style of Charlie Drake, "Hello my Darlings."

2. Writing your speech.

Pick a subject which you know about, or one which you feel passionate about. If you feel passionate about the subject, it usually helps. There is no point in choosing to speak about South American tree frogs if they do not interest you and you neither love nor loathe them. You would be better to choose a local issue to speak about, which you can back up with hard evidence. For an audience of local people, this subject

Page 3

is bound to hold their interest for longer than a South American tree frog anyway.

Ending your speech is equally important. You need to leave your audience and the judges with something to remember you by. An amusing anecdote related directly to your speech will stick in their minds, or a hard hitting quote, again related directly to the main body of your speech.

Your speech needs a strong opening, a factual, interesting middle, which doesn't contain too much waffle and finally a neat, memorable ending.

N.B. Tell them where you are going; tell them what you are telling them; tell them what you have told them.

3. Presentation is very important in public speaking in:

i) The terms you use. The opening of your speech needs to be neat and explain exactly what you are going to talk about. For example, "Tonight, ladies and gentlemen, I am going to talk to you about something very near to our hearts, lungs and livers – organ donation."

This opening gets straight to the point and catches the attention of the audience immediately. Of course, after a strong opening, the rest of the speech needs to have the same snappy style.

ii) The way you present yourself. When speaking in public, it is a good idea to go to the lectern if there is one. You can put your notes on it, hold on to it so you don't fall over with nerves and it hides your wobbly knees!

> Nice delivery dear, but you know the lectern won't hide everything.

The 1994 B.P.W.

This was my first public speaking competition. I had seen debates at the heats of the Hammond Suddard debating competition, but that was completely different. Debating is much more personal. By that I mean the speakers actually insult one another! Public speaking is a totally different kettle of fish. You are speaking with people you know, on a topic which you know a considerable amount about, and nobody is going to interrupt you. (Other teams don't interrupt you when debating, but I think that most of the time if they had the chance, some of the teams would be jumping down each others throats before the words were out, to argue their point.)

I took the part of the chair for our team. The chair person is in control of the meeting and introduces the main speaker and the expresser of thanks. My speech was about Anna, who was our main speaker. I think that I spoke for too long about her actually. I told the audience all kinds of things and now that I think about it that probably detracted from her speech which was quite long in any case!

The most nerve racking part of the meeting was when I had to open it to the floor. All questions have to be directed through the chair. Time management is also taken into consideration by the judges, so I had to cut one of the questions short, politely.

Our team didn't win. Not because we weren't good, just because the other Calder High team were better! However, Anna did win the award for best speaker and of course the important thing is that the trophy came back to Calder High!

The worst part of the evening was sitting, waiting nervously through all the other speeches. Some of them were interesting, but on the whole I didn't much enjoy enlightening speeches about Penalties, Juvenile Crime and Apartheid (not because I don't think that these issues are important, but the speakers were not particularly enthralling.)

Basically, speakers are not born, they learn, and I'm afraid that these girls were still learning, as was I. I learnt first of all that waffling doesn't do you any favours, secondly that I had to make it look as if it was

Page 5

the first time I had ever heard Anna's speech, not the hundredth, and that had she gone wrong I would have been able to take up where she left off! Finally, I learnt that the judges don't always make the decisions that you expect them to make, so you can never predict what the result is going to be.

As Thomas Jefferson once said:
"I'm a great believer in luck, and the harder I work, the more I have of it!"

Thanks! I hope I don't forget it all before I speak.

Bibliography and Further Reading

Painless Public Speaking. By Sharon Bower.

"Unaccustomed as I am." An article in a British Airways' Inflight magazine (February 1994).

"The Nervous Woman's Guide to Public Speaking." An article in Cosmopolitan (April 1994).

Page 6 (back)

iii) The spontaneity of your speech. Nobody expects you to have learnt your notes word for word. However don't go to the lectern with three sheets of A4 paper and read straight from them. It is a good idea to write your speech out on cards and join them by punching a hole in them and tying them together. If you think you can cope, only put a few notes on the cards, so that you are only referring to them, then you can make eye contact with the audience.

iv) The introduction of some humour. If your speech can amuse your audience, you will persuade them to your point more easily, gain more marks and enjoy yourself more, which is equally as important in speaking!

4. Five deadly sins of public speaking.

i) Sonorous monotones – if there is no variation in pitch or speed of your speech, the audience will simply lose interest. Speak slowly and clearly, vary the pitch of your speech, so that it sounds interesting. If the speech sounds interesting, your audience is more likely to listen to the words. It is, of course, all right to pause, find your place in your notes and carry on. Pausing will not lose you marks.

ii) Verbal gunfire – do not target your aggression at your audience. You are not lecturing them as if they were naughty school children. You are trying to win them over! Smile at them, being pleasant with your audience does not mean that you aren't serious.

iii) Shuffling feet – when you are nervous, it is natural to shift your weight from foot to foot. Don't do it! Stand absolutely still. Imagine your feet are set in concrete.

iv) Intimacy – eye contact is the most important factor of public speaking. You have to make your audience feel as if you are speaking to each one of them personally. Burying your head in your notes does not provoke audience participation or compel them to listen to what you have to say. Your aim must be to make eye contact with each person in the audience at least once during your speech.

v) More "ums" than a Lionel Richie chorus! – another big no-no for public speakers. Um syndrome. Too many ums upset the rhythm. Silent pauses are just fine and can add dramatically to your speech. Ums simply make your speech difficult to understand.

Page 4

TEXT 25

My Kind of Day

Lowri Turner
Looking Good
Tuesdays BBC2

❝I caught sight of my behind in the bathroom mirror the other week and thought, 'God, you could read this in braille', the cellulite was so bad. So now I'm running every morning, entirely in panic, to try to keep my thighs under control. They are looking better, if still a bit cart-horsey. I don't think I'll ever wear a mini-skirt.

I go through phases. I either keep really fit and eat healthily, or sit on the sofa and stuff chocolate chip ice cream and grow to the size of a small elephant. When I was a teenager I was big for my height (five foot) at size 14. But it's not a crime, it just made shopping for clothes a bit of a pain. I never had any problems with boyfriends.

I'm a triplet with one identical sister, Catrin. I've been known to walk up to a mirror and say, 'Hi, Catrin!' My other sister, Nerys, is mentally disabled and sometimes comes to stay. I'm very close to Catrin, although we did almost kill each other when we lived together. When you've shared more or less the same experiences for 32 years you tend to finish each other's sentences.

Catrin's a lawyer and is more conservative in her dress than I am, but we're the same size and borrow each other's clothes. She went on a diet before she got married so I did, too, and got down to size eight. It lasted until the reception. Now I keep three wardrobes – fat, thin and middling. It adds insult to injury if you grow out of a size and you've thrown away the clothes that would fit you.

My father was Welsh, which accounts for our names. I also have two brothers, Geraint and Glyn. But we were all brought up in north London and I prefer pavement to hillside. I live in a one-bedroom flat in a Regency terrace in Marylebone which I bought years ago when I was fashion editor of the London *Evening Standard* and was appearing on *Good Morning* with Anne and Nick. The mortgage is huge, but I don't have a car so it's important to be near a tube. The Bakerloo line runs directly underneath and you can hear and feel the rumble of the trains. Did the earth move for me? Yes, it did.

I live with my partner Paul Connew, a print journalist, and we wake up early. The papers are delivered with a thud at 6.45 – we have every paper, everyday – and it's straight into a Diet coke and the first cigarette. Tragic, isn't it? Then, looking absolutely hideous in black leggings, I'm off on the morning run, puffing past the llama in the children's section of London Zoo. It's the one time of day nobody can call me – I refuse to take my mobile.

My 'study' is the kitchen table and in a normal week I'll write features and prepare for my regular TV and radio shows – I review the papers on Wednesdays for Sky's *Sunrise*, have a spot on *Showbiz Weekly* and present the weekend morning shows for the London radio station 963 Liberty. I've also just finished a book on Gianni Versace. *Looking Good* is the fashion series I've always wanted to make – not supermodels on catwalks, but the real dilemmas that women face. It's very 'how to'.

Until the series I hadn't really bought any clothes for three years. I have two Calvin Klein suits which I bought cheaply in the Caribbean, but I have difficulty spending a lot on my wardrobe. As one of five kids, I was bought up on jumble sales and as I'm short I can fit into teenage gear. At weekends I usually look really rough – you can on radio. But if the going gets tough, I just put on another layer of make-up. I'm a great believer in lipstick.❞

Lowri Turner was talking to David Gillard
Next week: Jonathan Dimbleby

COMMENTARY You will probably have realised that one answer by the subject often leads to a supplementary question. The interviewer will be flexible in approach, having a number of questions prepared in order to give a starting point and provide back-up should one line of enquiry fade out or become uninteresting. This will allow the interviewee to lead the discussion if an unexpected aspect of his/her life is revealed.

ACTIVITY 22

Interview a friend or member of your family for a 'My Kind of Day' feature who you think leads an interesting life. Remember, your subject doesn't have to be a world famous sportsperson, pop-star or captain of industry to be interesting. Prepare your list of questions in advance but be prepared to follow any avenue which opens up if it seems this will provide you with good copy.

If your subject agrees, it would be a good idea to record the conversation so that you can be certain what was said. Arrange your material to its best advantage and write your article in the first person, trying to be true to what your subject has offered in the interview. You will have noticed from Text 25 that the subject does not stick to one particular day in her life.

As a matter of courtesy show your subject what you have written. Their comments might give

you some points for your commentary, especially if you redraft as a result.

One student interviewed her grandfather about his experiences in the Second World War and ended up with a powerful piece of writing, in the first person, dramatising the events of this part of his life. The student did not merely write out what her grandfather had told her as this would not have qualified as original writing, but used his memories as the basis for the central character who delivers a monologue. Notes taken during the conversation were included in an appendix to the piece and the differences between these and the finished piece of writing formed an impressive part of the commentary. Though this was not a 'My Kind of Day' piece, the techniques of preparation and interviewing which led to it were the same.

So far we have looked at writing which draws on the personal experience of writers or someone known to them. In the next type of writing you'll have to combine the techniques of writing to inform with research skills and rewriting a text for a particular audience. A good model for this is a series which ran in *The Sunday Times* entitled 'An Interview to Die For'. In this series the writers chose famous figures of the 20th century who are now dead and, having done the necessary background reading, conducted an imaginary interview with their subject.

The extract below is from the 'interview' with Jackie Onassis. There is a danger here that if the preparatory research is not extensive or thorough enough the main function of the piece will be to entertain rather than inform. In this extract you can see how Gina Howell's research is shown: there are the details for instance, of Jackie Onassis' wardrobe, her studies in France, winning the talent contest, working for the *Washington Times Herald* as a photographer/reporter. All these facts could be gleaned from reading a biography of Jackie Onassis but it is what Howell does with the facts she has researched which make it original.

TEXT 26

HOW TO MARRY A MILLIONAIRE

After Kennedy was assassinated, the public thought her a saint. Then she stunned the world by marrying a Greek shipping magnate for his money. In the sixth imaginary interview with a 20th-century icon, Georgina Howell meets the woman who became an American cult.

There was some sort of crisis going on that day in the fitting rooms of Chanel at 31 rue Cambon. We two women were marooned together for half an hour in satin armchairs in the claustrophobic private apartment of Chanel on the first floor, the air heady with No 5, hedged in between the black and gold Chinese screens with abject apologies, caviare and a bottle of vintage Bollinger. It was impossible not to say something.

I had arrived a few minutes before her, and I had seen the black Mercedes pull up with the two outriders, and the bodyguard sitting in front next to the chauffeur. The immaculate, doll-like figure in its pale pink tweed suit ran quickly up the steps, head down in huge sunglasses, a fur pillbox framing the wide face, a quilted bag swinging on its chain over the elbow-length white gloves. A few minutes later, the dragon-like *vendeuse* showed her in with me, positively writhing with apologies. The woman who walked in looked utterly familiar: it was as if Marilyn Monroe or Sophia Loren had stepped into the room. Could it really be ...

She took off her gloves and sunglasses, and threw them on the lacquer table. She glanced quickly at me from under her thick dark eyebrows, and her absurdly wide-set eyes were as black and shiny as boot buttons.

"Excuse me," I said hesitantly. "I expect people tell you the same thing all the time. You look so like ..."

She smiled, and her camellia-pink lips parted over even white teeth. Then she said in that breathy little girl voice, "Yes, I'm Jackie Onassis. I just had to come over for the spring collection. There's nowhere like Paris, is there?" I murmured something.

"Oh, Paris ..." she whispered. "I came here first from Vassar, to study French literature and history at the Sorbonne. It opened my eyes! The paintings, the antiques, the language, the museums and shops ..."

I remembered we had something in common. We had both won the Vogue Talent Contest, with the prize of a year's employment on the magazine – Jackie Bouvier in New York, me in London. I remembered that she had won it for her essay "People I wish I had known", choosing Oscar Wilde, Charles Baudelaire and Sergei Diaghilev. The difference was that I had jumped at the job, and Jackie had turned it down. "I didn't want to," she said in a small voice. "As a matter of fact, I was quite devastated. Daddy was all for it, but my mother put a stop to it. She thought it was undignified."

"Didn't you go to work for the Washington Times-Herald after that?"

She laughed. "That was a lot of fun. I earned $42.50 a week, and my title was Inquiring Photographer. I just walked around town with a camera and asked people questions, like 'Are men braver than women in the dentist's chair?' or 'Can you spot a married man?'

"But a job like that couldn't have been too different from the job you would have had on Vogue. So what made your mother agree to it?"

She took a sip of champagne, and hesitated. She set down the glass on the table as if she had decided to talk without reservation.

"You see, what it was, my mother hated my father. If I had taken the New York job, I would have been on daddy's doorstep. It was Hughdie who got me the Washington job – my mother had been married to him for nine years, then. So that was fine with Mother. I would be out of ... out of Daddy's reach."

What a match that had been for divorced, ambitious Janet Bouvier. Obtaining a quick divorce from "Black" Jack Bouvier in Reno, she swapped his harem of girlfriends and his $64,000 debts for the immense fortune of Hugh Auchincloss, an investment banker who inherited Standard Oil money from his mother, Emma Brewster Jennings.

He headed New York society through his family connections with the Vanderbilts, the Rockefellers, the Du Ponts, the Tiffanys and the Saltonstalls. He owned the 46-acre Merrywood estate in McLean, Virginia, where he spent the winters, and the 75-acre Hammersmith Farm in Newport, where he spent the summers. Each place had its Rolls Royces, its stables and tennis courts, its butlers and housekeepers and maids.

"Uncle Hughdie had been married twice before. His first wife was Gore Vidal's mother, you know."

"Did you like Hughdie?"

"He was pleasant ... he was kind of dull, actually. With all that money, he was mean about small things. I remember I left the light on in the bathroom one night, and he came and gave me a ticking off. And he had some real nasty books in his library ... My sister Lee and I had a look once, when he was away, and it was stuff that churned you up. Lee had nightmares about it."

"You were voted deb of the year, weren't you? I remember reading somewhere that your father wasn't invited to your coming-out ball at Newport – was that what you wanted?"

"No," she whispered. She fiddled nervously with the interlinked Cs of her handbag.

"That must have been your mother's work."

She nodded. "She arranged an 18th birthday dinner-dance at the Clambake Club for me and hundreds of my friends, with two bands and a marquee. Daddy was devastated not to be asked. He rang up Mother and gave her a real hard time about it, but she said he could give another party for me in New York any time he wanted. Of course, she knew a party paid for by Daddy simply couldn't compete."

"How awful for him to be written out of your life like that. How did that make you feel?"

Her nervousness increased. She looked down at her sapphire ring for a moment, and shifted in her chair. When she looked up again, her face was even paler, her black eyes moist.

"About D ... addy?" I noticed how, when she mentioned him, she stammered. Then she spoke in a rush. "I got awful letters from him all the time, you know. Terrible, imploring, doting letters accusing me of forgetting him, not loving him any more, selling out to the Auchinclosses. He was possessive about me to the point of paranoia.

At Farmington, the school where they sent me in Connecticut, he rang all the time, somethimes three times an evening. It was embarrassing. I used to dodge his calls. He always wanted me to come to him for the weekend. Sometimes he'd arrange to come and take me out, and I would bring three or four friends with me. They adored him ... he was so good-looking. He was always being mistaken for Clark Gable. He made us laugh, he took us to the best restaurant in Hartford, he treated us like grown-up women!" She stopped abruptly, picked up her gloves and began to twist them between her fingers.

> The potential for this type of assignment is vast. Imagine an interview with Alexander the Great for history students, an interview with Shakespeare for literature students or with James Dean for film buffs.

ACTIVITY 23

Choose a person you admire from history, music, literature, or whatever – the choice is yours – and conduct your own 'Interview to Die For'. When you write up your 'interview' remember to tailor it to the word count requirements of your course.

> *The Times* publishes on Saturdays a supplement called 'Metro'. This magazine carries a feature entitled 'The Vulture picks over the bones of contemporary culture' in which the writer(s) choose one music album, one book and one film and analyse their importance to modern popular culture. Though dealing with modern, popular culture the column is often erudite, making references which require at least some knowledge of the text or period being evaluated.

TEXT 27

GOING TO SEED? The Byrds in 1967

THE NOTORIOUS BYRD BROTHERS (1968)

In an ideal world, musicians would produce their greatest work in harmony with their fellow players, but often the reverse is true. By late 1967, the Byrds were in complete disarray. Midway through recording this album they unceremoniously fired their leading songwriter, David Crosby. His replacement was former-Byrd Gene Clark (fired the previous year), who lasted a mere three weeks and contributed nothing to this work. By the time the sessions had been completed, drummer Michael Clark was also dismissed.

What should have been a disjointed mess instead emerged as one of the most breaktaking albums of the era – a seamless mood piece and triumph of studio ingenuity.

Phasers, reversed tapes, Donald Duck brass, string sections and synthesizers were all used by producer Gary Usher to enhance the playing. Lyrically, the songs were equally imaginative: there was space rock (*Space Odyssey*), hippie philosophy (*Change is Now*), Vietnam protest (*Draft Morning*), drug exploration (*Artificial Energy*) and two Goffin/King compositons to complement the tranquil ambience. This ultimate exercise in pop *hara-kiri* prompted critics to joke whether Roger McGuinn and Chris Hillman would henceforth become a West Coast Simon and Garfunkel. Instead, they restructured the group, but for many this was the Byrds' glorious epitaph.

KITTY KELLEY – HIS WAY (1986)

Kitty Kelley's American publication of her *exposé* of the British royals soon after Diana's death, could not have been worse (or better) timed, and confirmed one half of her Jekyll and Hyde reputation –

that of the sensationalising, dirt-digging, ruthless paparazzo-style hackette.

Certainly Frank Sinatra saw her that way after she shot to fame, fortune and follow-ups with this *unauthorised* biography of Ol' Blue Eyes. Sinatra ranks with Elvis and Monroe in the pantheon of American popular culture, a national icon. But Kelley got digging, and despite accusations of lifting material and shoddy research, went to great lengths in her hunt for Sinatra's warts and all. In fact, if even one tenth of her material is true, it is hard to see how any honest account could ever have got authorisaton. The King of crooners emerges as a monster of egoism, a bullying, vain, capricious thug, fascinated by Mafiosi, who sued and abused everything he touched. How the American press gloated when Australian trade unionists forced him to apologise.

Kelley is a feverish writer in the middle-market tabloid mould, but the colourful anecdotes stack up faster than the chips in a Vegas casino. And she has never been successfully sued.

THE MALTESE FALCON (1941)

THIS WAS Warner Brothers' third go at filming Dashiel Hammett's 1930 novel – and the first under its proper name. The film industry has something to learn from this. Actors: do not, like George Raft, turn down a picture because it is the dirctor's first. The director may be a genius like John Huston and produce something like this, which fixed Bogart, Sydney Greenstreet and Peter Lorre in the public mind for ever (there are those who say that Huston's real talent was not for directing, but for casting). Filmmakers and studio bosses: do not be tempted to muck about with the material. Huston was sensible enough to be faithful to Hammett's plot and superb dialogue (unlike the previous two versions). The result is a film that still packs a punch – for we are more used to imagining Bogart as the decent, Chandleresque private eye. Hammett's Sam Spade was more morally ambiguous, and there is real mischief in Bogart's grin each time he outwits (or thinks he outwits) the other characters. This is grown-up stuff.

ACTIVITY 24

Look at the extract from 'The Vulture'.

1 In pairs, discuss what there is in the text that shows:

   a the writer assumes shared knowledge on the part of the reader of popular 20th – century culture?

   b an awareness of language change eg borrowings from other cultures or new coinages?

   c formal lexis?

2 Are there any other interesting uses of language?

COMMENTARY

You should have noticed the following features of the writer's language:

- The pun in the sub-heading 'Going to seed' (Byrdseed) which combined the group's name with a suggestion that at this point the group were past their best.
- A lexical group to do with music production: *phasers, reversed tapes* etc.
- The reference to Japanese ritual suicide hara-kiri.
- Mention of the 60s/70s pop duo Simon and Garfunkel – perhaps an indicator of the age group being aimed at.
- Use of formal lexis: *icon, pantheon, epitaph, capricious* etc.
- Despite the point above a degree of informality is injected by the use of phrases such as *warts and all* and *This is grown up stuff*.
- Use of heavy pre-modification as in *sensationalising, dirt digging, ruthless, paparazzo-style hackette* and *bullying, vain, capricious thug*.
- There are neologisms (new coinages) such as *hackette*, an example of language borrowing, ie *paparazzo*.
- The writer also assumes knowledge of a particular culture, eg that Frank Sinatra's nickname was 'Ol' Blue Eyes'. This is especially true of the section on *The Maltese Falcon* in which names of people connected with the film are mentioned with little or no explanation.
- Either deliberately or unconsciously, the writer has used an alliterative phrase and alliteration always gives a piece a 'bounce'. This is found in the section *Kitty Kelley – His Way* in which Sinatra is referred to as 'King of Crooners' and the writer is described as being in the 'middle market tabloid mould'.

Let's play games!

Devising a board game which must have clearly explained rules in order for players to attempt the game successfully is a good exercise in writing clearly and informatively. If you do this, you must ensure that your game has been thoroughly tested so that its rules are crystal clear.

Below is one that a group of students successfully devised and developed. The task was to devise a spelling game which could be used with Year 7 pupils who attended a Spelling Club. The rules had to be clear and easy to follow. As the pupils had enjoyed the book *Mr Biff the Boxer* by Allan and Janet Ahlberg, the students decided to use this as the basis for their game. Skills other than writing were involved, for example the building of the model boxing ring which sat in the middle of the board and counters in the shape of boxers which players moved around the board. The game could be played without adult help and was greatly enjoyed.

TEXT 28

The students constructed, not a traditional die, but a pyramid with three faces numbered 1, 2 and 3, one face with a question mark and one face with a large letter 'S'. The players threw the pyramid to make progress round the game board. These were the rules that the students wrote:

1   The aim of the game is to get to the boxing ring and answer two questions correctly.
2   When the pyramid lands upright ie with the 'S' hidden, pick up an 'S' square. If the pyramid lands with a number on the top face move your boxer that number of places.
3   You move around the game answering questions on the book (Q) and sound, sight and sum questions (S).
4   The question cards ask questions about the book *Mr Biff the Boxer.* You must try to answer the question but if you can't the card will tell you what to do.
5   If you have to pick up a card then the person you are playing against must pick it up for you in case it is a spelling question.

The questions that were asked about the book tested that the children had understood it. For example, where was the boxing match held? A – a tent, B – a building, C – a field. If correct, move forward 4, if not, move back 4.

Landing on a 'S' space required the player to spell a word used in the book, eg Champion or Referee. 'S' spaces could also lead to a 'sums' question or a question on sounds, such as, 'Give 5 words with the "ee" sound', or, 'Give a word that rhymes with "talked"'. The students posed these questions for the children because their work for A-Level English Language had taught them the importance of children appreciating rhyme and its relation to their reading development. One of the beauties of this game which led to it being so popular was that once the basic rules printed above were understood, the wording on the game board itself or on the cards which had to be picked up guided the players through it. It was not a case of reading a complex 'rules of the game booklet' before starting the game.

ACTIVITY 25

1   Devise a board game of your own together with a set of rules. Remember that there are a number of conventions to follow. Of course, you might hit on a completely new format – in which case submit it to a games manufacturer. The board game should have a 'route' and an ultimate aim. In *Trivial Pursuit* this is the progression round the circular route answering questions, picking up a full set of wedges prior to landing on the centre spot and successfully answering a question. In *Cluedo* players move from room to room by throwing a die and asking questions to eliminate murder suspects, find the murder weapon and deduce which room the murder took place in.

- The most usual method of moving is to use a die/dice.
- Players are represented by counters, models or something similar.
- There are some board games however which do not use dice but rely on players continuing a series of shapes, colours or letters, eg *Scrabble*, but you'll find it easier to devise games which follow traditional lines.

The power of the Press

Have you ever wanted to be a journalist? In this next section you'll find the advice given to A-Level English Language students by the editor of a large circulation regional newspaper. He explained what he looked for when considering contributions.

TEXT 29

Spend as much time choosing what you want to write about and what you plan to say as much as you do writing the article. NEVER pad out your masterpiece or include waffle. Your aim is to produce quality not quantity. Waffle stands out a mile, doesn't contribute to the main message, irritates the reader and spoils the flow. Think of your skills of précis and shed all superfluous matter. Be sharp, be direct, be amusing if the subject allows and above all be adventurous with your English. We get away with it weekly by calling it journalese – as though it's halfway between what we should do grammatically and what we want to do – and we love these hyphen breaks I've just used.

Your first paragraph, which journalists call an intro, is vital. It is your shop window to sell all that follows and if it fails in its task the rest of what you write will have entertained, informed or persuaded you only. No one else will have read the piece.

Try to think in a mood that's appropriate to the piece and your writing will have an extra depth.

Do not be afraid of scrapping a paragraph if it does not reflect what you're trying to say.

Remember that in a general newspaper article you are aiming to appeal to the lowest common denominator. Use simple, non-complex language. Your style and the flow of the article will make up for any shortage of long words. A nice, simple turn of phrase is a joy to read (and edit).

You can choose your own subject but bear in mind its relevance to local issues. If you can cope with controversy then pick a controversial topic. There are so many!

Remember that a local newspaper needs to provoke a response and if an article generates many letters it is seen as a success.

ACTIVITY 26

Choose a topic of local interest and write an article for submission to your local newspaper. Prepare for the article by looking at ones that have appeared in your chosen paper. You should gauge the typical length of articles, the vocabulary level used, the complexity of sentence construction. Look for examples of preferred 'journalese' and see whether or not there is a distinct 'house style'.

Some possible topics for your article include:

- the need for a Park and Ride Scheme in your area
- days out on £10 of petrol
- the lack of facilities for young people/senior citizens in your locality
- what can be done about the litter in your town or city.

Something in the air

Do not think that you are limited to producing printed texts. Radio can also be used to inform, advise and explain. *The Archers* began as a radio drama which had as a secondary aim the dissemination of technical advice to farmers.

BBC Radio Five, before it became purely a news and sport network, was aimed at a young audience, broadcasting drama, current affairs and arts programmes. One informative series was *A Student Guide to...* and the presenter went to various university towns where he recorded the views of students, described the town and discussed issues such as housing, teaching quality and leisure facilities. What is interesting is that while the medium is different, there are parallels between written and printed texts. The table below shows how a radio show equates to a printed text.

PRINT	RADIO
Headings, sub-heads, illustrations to break up text.	Titles, musical links to give 'texture' in sound.
Quotation, changes of tone and register.	Sound bites, vox pops.
Paragraphing, tables, graphs, different fonts.	Voices differing by sex, accent and tone to add variety.
Language matched to audience.	Language matched to audience.
Scene setting, either in words or by use of photographs etc.	Scene setting by description, eg 'We're here in leafy Orwell Road in …'

ACTIVITY 27

Write an extract from a radio script to introduce a stranger to your town. Refer to the section on writing for radio for layout.

■ Think about the sounds which could suggest your town or city. Does it have a famous football team? A racecourse? A specific

industry? All these could provide interesting sounds.

■ Who would you interview to represent your town and what questions would you ask them?

Rounding off

This section by no means covers everything that can be offered in the categories of information, advice and explanation, but let us round off by summarising the techniques you might choose from. Remember that what follows is not meant to be a checklist against your own writing as checklists can lead to 'deficit model' commentaries in which you say what you haven't done.

You will notice that some of these points are also featured in other types of writing. This is inevitable as many pieces of writing fulfil more than one purpose, but if your primary purpose is not compromised this should not be a problem.

As with any piece of writing, whatever its purpose, the correct register for the target audience should be used. This might be shown by the use of peer group language or technical terms. You can draw attention to this in your commentary.

■ Give a clear heading/title. Use sub-heads if suitable. These should be related to the heading or title by being part of the same lexical group.
■ Use white space to avoid large, off-putting text blocks.
■ Offer data in the form of charts, graphs, 'expert' testimony etc.
■ Use bullet points.
■ Use recognisable symbols such as the Kitemark, logos etc.
■ Provide the option for audience involvement through questionnaires/tick-boxes.
■ Use the Question/Answer format.
■ Remember that illustrations, photos and cartoons add variety and interest.

- Use colour to emphasise.
- Use different fonts and print sizes to attract the eye of the reader.
- Linguistic 'tricks' such as alliterative phrases, slogans etc aid reader memory.
- Have a clear 'controlling idea', ie what information do you want to impart?
- Give details for the reader to gain further information if necessary, such as addresses, names, telephone numbers.
- Use a direct form of address to draw the reader in.
- Humour can be useful to make a point.

Finally, a general point, whatever the subject or the audience: the information, advice or explanation should be as clear as possible.

Student's Commentary on Text 24

The idea for a leaflet about public speaking was born when I was asked to speak at a prospective parent's evening at the beginning of my lower sixth year. From that speech, I realised that it is a nerve-wracking experience and lots of preparation is necessary! Further thinking made me want to help future speakers in the sixth form to keep up the good reputation the school has in both public speaking and debating competitions in this area.

A leaflet seemed to be the best way to present the information, because that way the information isn't particularly overpowering, yet it can be equally as direct and useful as an essay or article for a paper or magazine. A leaflet for use within school also has the advantage of being able to be patriotic about the school's past successes, as well as poke a little fun at the people involved in the preparation of the competition, through both the language used and the cartoons, which also break up the text and help to keep the reader's interest.

My main purpose for writing the leaflet was to instruct future competitors in public speaking competitions on the best way to go about writing and presenting a speech, and the majority of the leaflet is devoted to that, however I also decided to include some of my own experiences, which adds elements of information and humour to the leaflet.

The language I have used is informal in the introduction and my own experience of the 1994 B.P.W., for example, in the introduction I chose to say "This comprehensive guide ..." to indicate not only that that is what I hope it to be, but that it is factual. The rest of the introduction has a more easy going tone, with comments on the school's previous performances and a little sarcasm, so as not to frighten new speakers completely away from the idea! In the main body of the leaflet – that is the instruction of how to go about successful public speaking – I used a much more formal style, yet still keeping the tone on a personal level by using the pronoun 'you' and keeping a little humour throughout.

In order to make sure preparation goes according to plan in the few weeks running up to a competition, it was of course important to write the leaflet in the correct order. I have tried to include useful pointers such as the suggestion that sex and politics aren't good topics for a competition like the B.P.W., and ideas of styles which the speaker could adopt as far as presentation is concerned. I found that to encourage my readers to take this point of humour on board, that I would introduce a similar form of humour into my own leaflet. This progression can be seen in the drafts included, particularly in the section about The Five Deadly Sins of Public Speaking.

The audience is intended to be members of the lower sixth who are preparing for public speaking competitions, and as I also entered the 1995 B.P.W. with a member of the lower sixth as the chair in our team, I tried the leaflet out on her. She found the leaflet very helpful, and said that there was a good balance between humour and hard information. She commented that the layout made it easy to read, and above all, she said that after reading the leaflet, she felt more confident because she knew more of what to expect! Which was just as well, because our team in the 1995 B.P.W. went through to the next round, with me as the main speaker.

5 Writing a Commentary

In this section we shall be looking at what makes a successful commentary. We will start by looking at some poems submitted as coursework and the commentaries which went with them.

You will notice that commentaries on poems tend to be longer than the poems themselves. If you keep notes on where your ideas came from, how you developed the poems through drafts, made conscious decisions about language choice and any reader reaction, you will have everything you need to write a full and illuminating commentary.

In each case, the poems printed below were from collections offered by the students as it really takes a range of poetry to show your ability. All the poems are followed by moderator's notes explaining how the commentary has succeeded and how it might have been improved.

TEXT 30

Wedding Album

One from the Stag Night,
tinged with Autumnal brown,
thanks to the prat who threw
his pint over the cameraman.
The groom whips off his pants,
along with fourteen other newts,
as the best man pukes over his dad.

That forest is dark,
with blackened trees, dark and sinister.
In the midst of the gloom,
shines a worried groom,
as he wonders where his clothes are.

The askance groom,
accompanied by his hangover,
stands uncertainly.
Prospective mother-in-law
glowers intently,
and the best man
throws up profusely.

Team photo vicar picks his nose,
the bridesmaid belts the page,
a pale groom watches as the
best man disappears from the frame,
as the new mothers-in-law slang it out.

The bride, trying to be radiant,
realises her train is in the mud.

In the out-of-focus reception,
the cake, four tiers,
falls to the floor,
courtesy of an inebriated uncle.
The hippoesque Auntie Joan
dismantles her fourth jam sponge,
as the best man performs his party trick,
over your photographer.

Candidate's Commentary on 'Wedding Album'

'Wedding Album' was written after a family wedding and the poem was an attempt to suggest the chaos of a stag night and the wedding the following day.

There are a few running jokes to give the whole thing a unity. These are partly concerned with the groom's appearance and attitude. He is described with the neutral 'the groom' but is also 'a worried groom', 'the askance groom' and 'the pale groom'. The best man's drunkenness has been treated with poetic licence so that he is made to throw up on several occasions, all of them inappropriate.

I referred to the stereotypical behaviour of 'lads' on a stag night; throwing beer about, removing their trousers and abandoning the groom in a remote spot without his clothes. There are other stereotypical ideas in the poem – the hostile prospective mother-in-law who 'glowers', the children who get bored and fight instead of standing still for photographs, a drunken uncle who destroys the wedding cake and a large auntie who enjoys her food and ignores the other goings on at the reception.

The language of the poem is quite informal and colloquial. The young man who threw a pint over the photographer as he was taking a shot of the group so that beer acted as a filter turning the photo 'Autumnal brown' is referred to as 'the prat'. The whole group on the stag night is referred to as 'newts' after the small amphibian famed, for some reason, for its drunkenness.

Group photos at weddings always remind me of football team photos. In the fourth stanza the team photo shows the vicar picking his nose.

The bridesmaid 'belts' the page.

There were some attempts to use language in an unusual way. The groom is described as 'askance' in an attempt to suggest that he is uncomfortable (and hungover) under the scrutiny of his soon to be mother-in-law and won't look at her directly. The word 'prolific' is usually complimentary, as in 'prolific goalscorer' or 'prolific novelist' but here it is used to point out that the best man is continually throwing up. Auntie Joan is described as 'hippoesque'. Large women are often described as 'Junoesque', which suggests grace and beauty. This Auntie Joan is more like a hippopotamus than a goddess and the word 'dismantled' rather than 'eats' is meant to suggest that she takes apart her sponge cakes in an almost mechanical way before devouring them.

It is a cliché that brides are radiant but in the poem her radiance is somewhat lessened by the fact that her train is in the mud.

The structure of the poem is quite loose. Three of the five stanzas have seven lines but that is coincidence rather than design. There is no regular rhyme scheme, but in stanza two gloom and groom are rhymed. This is to draw attention to his plight. His pale, naked body is shining in the forest where his friends have abandoned him.

In the last stanza the phrase 'out of focus reception' is intended to be ambiguous. It could be out of focus because the photographer doesn't really know how to take pictures or because the guests have drunk so much that they are having trouble seeing clearly.

This poem was written to amuse by including as many mishaps that could happen at one wedding as possible, and by exaggerating the tensions of the event. People who read it did seem to find it amusing and some said that some of the incidents included had happened at weddings they'd been to.

Moderator's report

This candidate gives a clear idea of the intentions behind the writing of the poem. It is to amuse. The writer states that it has been read by an appreciative audience, but does not explain whether any earlier drafts were shown and whether reader reaction led to any re-writing.

The origins of the poem are also made clear, the poem was inspired by the events of a family wedding.

The writer mentions using 'poetic licence' (departing from the facts for an effect) when exaggerating the best man's drunken behaviour and explains that this is done to pull the poem together, as are the descriptions of the groom given at various points.

The writer also draws on shared ideas, ie the 'stereotypical behaviour' of young men on a stag night. This shows awareness of audience and makes the poem accessible for those not involved in the events which inspired the poem. He refers to other stereotypes used for humorous effect which add to the overall tone of the poem.

The writer explains that the language used is informal, giving examples to illustrate this. He picks on particular words which were chosen because they might not be the obvious ones to choose, e.g. 'askance' and 'prolific' are picked out and their use explained.

The writer explains how he came to use the word 'hippoesque', though there is no indication that he is aware that he might have invented this word for the purposes of the poem.

The form of the poem is also commented on with the honest admission that the stanzas are as they are by accident rather than design.

This commentary does have a weakness; it is that changes from draft to draft until the final version was arrived at are not catalogued, the opportunity to illuminate the process of writing has therefore been lost. However, in terms of successfully amusing the intended audience, there can be no doubt that 'Wedding Album' achieves the poet's aim.

The following poem is one of many written by this student during her course. It is included because of the way details have been observed and reproduced in the poem which was written years after the incident on which it was based took place.

TEXT 31

Unattended Café

Waiting for the waitress
the child could have seen
the melted butter smeared on the plastic counter,
the flies buzzing over the damp, hot sugar,
the greying aprons hung from rusty hooks
and the mug of scummy water
in which they kept the scoop warm.
But instead
he saw the raftered ceiling.
And he watched his cracked flip-flop scuff the floor
as he tried to remember the French
for
Chocolate ice cream.

Commentary on 'Unattended Café'

This poem is based on something which happened on a family holiday in France years ago. The 'child' is my brother and we had gone into a café while driving to our campsite. It was a very basic establishment and not particularly clean. For a long time no one appeared to serve us. My brother was determined to order his own ice cream and went to the counter. Details of the café are given but the boy waiting to be served didn't notice any of its unpleasant aspects, nor the fact that he was being watched as he looked up at the ceiling and down at the floor in the effort to remember his French lessons.

The details described are genuine and slightly distasteful – the smeared butter, the flies over the sugar and the mug of scummy water – but the boy doesn't notice them.

The repetition of 'wait' in the opening line 'Waiting for the waitress' was intended to be ironic – we were expecting to be waited on; she made us wait. In the first few drafts this line was 'waiting to be served' but I liked the repetition of 'wait' when I was trying different phrases and retained this in the final version.

Also in earlier drafts there were non-specific insects buzzing around but I decided that if I said they were 'flies' the reader might be able to visualise them more clearly.

Early drafts also tended to be a bit short of adjectives. The first draft began:
    'Waiting to be served the child could have seen
    the butter smeared on the counter ...'
I felt that the addition of 'melted' and 'plastic' made the events more concrete.

Use of 'the child' and 'he' instead of a name was used to make the poem less specific to one family.

This seemed a nice, self-contained subject for a poem but there are no deliberately poetic techniques used here, though I did play with the length and layout of lines till I arrived at a version I was satisfied with.

Moderator's report
Here is a writer who is obviously aware of the effects words can have on the tone of a piece and the reader's understanding of it. The writer carefully explains why certain words were chosen over others or added to the drafts.

As with 'Wedding Album', the inspiration for the poem is clearly established, as is the character whose behaviour it is based on.

While this is obviously the work of an accomplished writer the commentary might have been improved if the writer had explained why the final arrangement of lines was chosen.

There is no mention of the audience for this piece but it was written for, and published in, a school anthology, a point the writer could have made, especially given that the vast majority of the readers would be between 11 and 18 years of age. It would have been interesting to read what the writer's younger brother thought of this account of the incident.

TEXT 32

The next poem, 'Phil', won the Wordsworth – British Gas poetry competition in the 16–18 year old category.

Phil
We are shown to our table. We sit and smile pleasantly and falsely.
Someone mentions the delightful swan carved from ice
Sitting gracefully on an elegant lace table cover.
The swan is duly admired and then we
Plunge back into silence with our rehearsed, nervous, apologetic smiles.
Except for Phil.
During the course of the meal
We will have a little to drink and we will
Comment on the food and criticise the service.
Phil won't.
Secretly, we all admire Phil;
It's 8 o'clock and he's completely pissed on Smirnoff.

He waves the empty vodka bottle expressively as he confides in me with
His most considered opinions. He asks, 'Do you know that
You've got the sexiest body I've ever seen?'
I go red, Darren looks deadly.
Phil then turns to Catherine [on his right] and says,
'You know what. You've got the sexiest body I've ever seen.' In what he
Supposes is a whisper. Catherine frantically turns to John.
John looks deadly. Darren looks deadly. John looks at Darren.
Darren looks at John. They both glare at Phil. Phil just grins.

Phil is marvellously unaware of the commotion he's causing;
Waitresses giggle while the head waiter and deputies gather in council.
Catherine joins Darren and John in being furious.
I just stare at the quietly congealing chicken and bite my lip.
Then, Phil farts, loudly.
He flings out his arms and knocks over the bottle of wine.
I laugh, Phil laughs, Kate cries – her dress is ruined.
The entire restaurant is staring at us.
Darren and John are so intense I swear they're going to kill Phil.
The angry looks silence us all for a moment.
And then, as if cued by some invisible director,
There is a terrible crack. In the cold silence of the frowning restaurant,
It's like a pistol firing.
Attention is flung to the beautiful ice sculpture whose head falls off
And shatters on the floor.

The headless swan sits grotesquely on its table
And we all linger a while in suspended animation.
Until a grin forms on my darling's face.
He tries to suppress it but he just can't stop it.
He begins to snigger, John follows suit.
Snigger turns to giggle which in turn turns to hysterics.

Even Kate cannot fail to see the hilarious situation.
And so the five of us weep with laughter.
And all thanks to Phil for reminding us
We don't need to play grown-ups yet.

Commentary on 'Phil'

This poem was written after a meal out to celebrate someone's A-Level results. It was quite a formal occasion at an up-market hotel restaurant and we were a bit over-awed by the place.

The events of the poem are just as they happened in reality – not even the names have been changed to protect the innocent. I did toy with the idea of writing this as a short story but I enjoy writing poetry and I thought that if I condensed the events into this relatively short poem it might be more dramatic and (hopefully) amusing.

I wrote in the first person and tried to provide details which would help a reader visualise the scene eg:
> '... the delightful swan carved from ice
> sitting gracefully on an elegant lace table cover.'

This serves two purposes:
a)   To put the idea of the swan in the reader's mind
b)   To suggest the formality and 'poshness' of the place

I hoped that lines such as:
> 'We are shown to our table. We sit and smile pleasantly and falsely'

might be read as one would read a film script. I think I was unconsciously remembering the opening scene of the film 'Goodfellas' when I wrote this.

The present tense is used throughout except for a short section when the future is used. This is to create the idea of immediacy. The only person named in the first stanza is Phil. This seemed appropriate as he is the 'star' of the situation.

In the second stanza the short, staccato phrases are an attempt to mirror the tension when Phil tells two of the girls that they have 'the sexiest body I've ever seen'.

In stanza three fun is poked at the head waiter and his deputies by suggesting that they 'gather in council' as if they are an important body of people (which in their own minds they undoubtedly are).

The chicken is described as 'quietly congealing'. These words were chosen because congealing means to become stiff or solid with cold and this is just what was happening to the atmosphere. Till Phil farts.

Though this really happened it is an old tradition of English humour. Geoffrey Chaucer's Absolon does it in 'The Miller's Tale' to great effect and it would weaken the poem if this wasn't included. To paraphrase Chaucer in the Miller's Prologue, 'I must tell their tales whether they are decent or not or else falsify my report.'

The only other 'off-colour' reference in the poem is in the first stanza where Phil is described as 'pissed'. Given the audience this poem was originally written for I did not feel this would cause offence.

The scene turns to one of slapstick as the wine bottle is spilled over a dress, the other diners stare and then the ice swan's head falls off. After the pause, there is laughter, which defuses the situation and brings a wave of relief.

There is one obvious linguistic device – the use of metonomy ie 'the frowning restaurant'. The restaurant cannot itself frown but the phrase suggests that this is what all the other diners are doing.

It did occur to me that a reader might be confused by the references to Catherine and Kate, not realising they are the same person, but left it as I originally wrote it as the people involved would know what I meant and anyone else could work it out if it was that important.

At first I thought the poem would only interest the group or others who knew the people involved but my English teacher said he'd enjoyed it and thought it would appeal to a wider audience.

[*Author's note*: the student's very detailed record of changes between drafts has not been included in this abridged commentary.]

Moderator's report

A good commentary can lift the mark of a flawed piece of writing if the student can demonstrate that he or she is fully aware of the effect of the language chosen. It could be said that the original commentary is so long that it reveals some insecurity on the part of the writer but it is more likely that, having been persuaded to reveal the poem to a wider audience than originally intended, she felt that a long and detailed commentary was necessary. Having said this, the commentary is not merely anecdotal – there is an obvious sense of purpose and engagement with the material and the process of writing.

Once again we see the strength that can be got from basing a poem on 'real' events or people, and the writer establishes this at the start of the commentary.

The reasons for presenting this as a poem rather than a short story are also considered. (The writer might have said that the events of the poem would have a made a short, amusing anecdote rather than a story).

Choices regarding vocabulary are carefully explained, the candidate even giving a justification of the 'taboo' language used ie that the original intended audience would not have objected.

The structure of the poem is carefully explained, as are any other factors eg the film 'Goodfellas' which might have influenced this.

There is a suitable amount of linguistic analysis and the writer avoids the trap which many student poets fall into, ie they feel that they have to give a line by line account of the process of constructing the poem. This writer gives more than enough evidence that she knows exactly what she's doing, while the drafts demonstrated a thoughtful, intelligent approach to the task of writing a poem and aiming it at a particular audience.

> The next poem was written by a mature student. It is included because it is more obviously 'poetic' than the three poems presented above. In fact, in one section of the commentary the student refers to some 'rather self-conscious use of alliteration'.

TEXT 33

Blue Sparks

My grandfather built ships.
Great grey giants that groaned
and grated their backward way
into the muddy embrace of the Mersey.

The blue sparks leaping from his torch
danced to the music of hammer and riveter
as he laboured, Hephaestus in a boiler suit,
amid the creative clangour
not knowing it was making him deaf.

Those powerful blue-scarred hands could
throw and catch me
as gently as the butterflies
landing on his cabbages.

That huge voice could
whisper conspiratorially as he gave me,
'Strong beer. Don't tell your mother!'

He loved the brown surging river
and stood at the Pier Head,
identifying flags and funnels.
Ships' names became an epic poem
told by a deaf Homer.

In retirement he continued,
in a pre-fab's confining yard,
fashioning a clinker-built boat.
but lacking the blue spark it languished on the stocks,
a skeletal monument to his skill,
until he died.

He told me once it was for a viking's funeral.
It would have been more fitting
than a box
silently sliding on greased rollers
through satin curtains.

Commentary on 'Blue Sparks'

This poem was written as a tribute to my grandfather after his death. He had been a boiler-maker since leaving school working in the shipyards of Liverpool and Birkenhead. [*Author's note* – a boiler-maker was originally someone who worked at riveting together the wrought-iron vessels used in steam engines. This term was later applied to craftsmen who used arc-welders as well as the traditional riveters].

He suffered from what is now known to be industrial deafness though at the time it was assumed to be hereditary – his younger son, also a boiler-maker, suffered from deafness too.

Because of his deafness and reluctance to wear his hearing-aid, my grandfather often spoke very loudly. He was, because of the physical nature of his job, very strong and muscular. He seemed to me to be a giant.

When he retired he began to work on a clinker built boat in the small back yard of his pre-fab. He died before it was finished. [*Author's note* – a clinker-built boat is one in which the external planks overlap each other below and are fastened with clinched copper nails. A pre-fab was a bungalow made of prefabricated sections which could be assembled quickly. Many were erected during and after the Second World War as temporary dwellings and some are still lived in today.]

In the early drafts the poem was called 'My Grandfather Built Ships' but I changed this to 'Blue Sparks' because I thought it sounded better and I had in mind the 'spark of creativity' as well as the blue sparks which are the result of oxy-acetylene welding.

As I looked up to my grandfather I tried to have a heroic theme in the poem. For this reason I compared him to Hephaestus, the Greek god of fire who forged weapons for the gods (he had sometimes worked round the clock during the war repairing ships needed for the war effort) and Homer, the Greek author of 'The Iliad' and 'The Odyssey'. The difference was that my grandfather was deaf while Homer was blind. There is also the reference to a Viking funeral in which a dead warrior is put into his long boat before it was set alight and pushed out to sea.

The poem begins with the straightforward declarative statement, 'My grandfather built ships.' There is then a rather self-conscious use of alliteration in,

>'Great grey giants that groaned
>and grated . . .'

The line was directly inspired by lines from the Wilfred Owen poem 'Strange Meeting':

>'. . .scooped
>Through granites which titanic wars had groined,
>Yet also there encumbered sleepers groaned'

I was told that the alliterated hard 'g' sound suggested the effort involved and decided to imitate the effect. In my first draft the line was,

>'. . . and grated their backward way down
>iron slipways'

but I didn't like the repetition of 'way' and thought the unconscious repetition of 'w' would overload the lines.

In stanza two I used alliteration again in the phrase 'creative clangour', hoping this would hint at the noisy chaos of a shipyard.

I tried to show the contrast of a powerful man with the gentle grandfather who grew vegetables and gave me sips of cider after first making sure my mother and grandmother were not around.

For the first two drafts there was a stanza explaining how he used to keep hens and, as I liked to collect the eggs and was rarely able to, he used to hide a pot egg in the straw of the hen house for me to find. I dropped this section as it didn't really add anything to the effect I wanted. [*Author's note* – a pot egg is a ceramic egg which owners would leave in the straw of the hen house to encourage the hens to lay].

His was the first cremation I attended and I thought of linking this to his 'Viking ship' and the sparks of welding. I'm not sure I made this link successfully and if I wrote further drafts would probably do further work on this last stanza.

Though I wrote the poem for no specific audience except myself I was pleased that my father and his brother thought enough of it to ask for copies.

Moderator's report

This is obviously a very personal poem and the motivation to write it is stated at the start of the commentary. The audience is a very small one, in the first instance the writer himself but as the writer's father and uncle asked for copies it is implied that there was audience approval, even if this was too late to cause any revisions.

There is no explanation of some of the specialised terminology used in the poem and this could be seen as a minor weakness.

The writer is making decisions about language which are reflected in the poem and explained in the commentary. Apart from the reference to alliteration noted in the introduction to this piece the writer also mentions the use of 'creative clangour' and the impression he hoped it would make.

The references to classical figures and their relevance to the subject of the poem are clearly described. The writer is aware of the exaggeration in these comparisons but explains that he wished to reflect the image of his grandfather as a hero.

The change of title to 'Blue Sparks' from 'My Grandfather Built Ships' is also justified and shows a creative imagination at work.

The writer refers to dropping a stanza at some stage in the development of the poem as it served no purpose.

Near the end of the poem the writer states that if time allowed he would have liked to work on the section which mentions the Viking funeral. It is not a weakness to admit that there are flaws in your work but only if there is evidence that a certain amount of effort has been expended on getting to where you are with the piece. It is unlikely to cut any ice with your teachers if there are no drafts to show that you have been attempting to improve and polish your work.

Before we consider the commentaries as a whole let us consider what can be learned about writing poetry from this section.

- Anything can be the subject of a poem; from small intimate events to universal themes.
- Poems do not spring perfectly formed from the writer's imagination but need revision and polishing.
- Poetry does not have to rhyme. For some writers the attempt to rhyme can lead to the problem of using a rhyme which doesn't suit the tone of the poem.
- Poetry doesn't have to follow the rules of punctuation and grammar.
- Sometimes a poem can be more successful than a story as a way of relating an incident.
- If you use a poetic device you must explain why you did this. It is not enough to say, 'I used alliteration.' The moderator will reply, 'So what?'
- Well-observed details of place or dialogue can give a poem depth and texture just as they can in a story or a play.

This next example of student writing and a commentary belongs in the 'writing to inform' category, but once again shows the importance of personal engagement with the topic.

TEXT 34

Clothes Show Live!

The atmosphere is electric. The lights lower. The audience grows quiet. Everyone is silent in anticipation. We wait for the moment to arrive. When it does, it's worth every minute of the wait.

The lights shine – the music blares and the show swings into action. Miss Naomi [Supermodel, renowned superbitch and superich] Campbell prowls down the catwalk sporting little more than a boob tube and a G-string, followed by the other hip-swingers, equally undressed in their Gaultier bras and Montana skirts.

Where are we? Paris? Milan? New York? No! We're in downtown Birmingham at the NEC for 'Clothes Show Live'.

'Clothes Show Live' has been running for years now. The amount of organisation that goes into the show is amazing. The fashion theatre itself covers a space bigger than half of Wembley Arena. It takes over 100 people to produce the show, and the models, who will have had their hair and make-up checked 14000 times by the end of the week and will have walked over 30 miles each. No wonder they're so thin!

Picture this scene – blacks, whites and reds flood the theatre as devils and angels mix, separate, to disappear on the misty platform which mysteriously lowers and rises several times throughout the show, to carry away from or deliver to the awestruck audience, the models.

Fancy yourself as the new Cindy, Linda or Christy?

Talent Scouts

Talent scouts will be touring the auditorium looking for new faces – or so the programme says. That must explain the variety of fashions on show; from grunge to rave; from 60s to 90s. It's all here and there's no missing the diversity. It's one of the great attractions.

Imagine yourself moving out of the fashion theatre. You're confronted by the absolute vastness of the NEC. It's time to invest in a programme complete with a map. At £3.00 it's not exactly a snip, but worth it if you want to have any idea of where you are or where you're going.

Hundreds of stalls

Wander through the hundreds of stalls [357 to be exact] and you'll realise you can find every type of style-monger here. The variety of clothes on view is immense. Move through bridal and lingerie sections to find make-up chic and cheap, Paco Rabane and CSL for men, underwear to outerwear, footwear to headgear – nothing has been left out.

Make-overs and hair-overs are available; some free, some not. Some for women, some for men. You can even have your face on the front cover of the Clothes Show magazine for 40 quid. Seems quite steep but the guide book tells you that hundreds will surrender themselves to the scissors.

For Men Too

Clothes Show Live for Men is in its 5th year now. It's immensely popular and always crowded out . . . but not with men! The male models may not have the grace and beauty of the woman but seeing as they're 'So damn horny' it doesn't seem to matter.

This is where the men's make-overs, and men's perfumes [sorry, fragrances] can be found. The companies whose stalls surround the catwalk have supplied the clothes. There's a 'Be a male model' competition and fitness demonstrations – after the dancing demonstrations.

There are thousands of freebies and a chance to win a car.

If that's not enough you also get to meet 'Top of the Pops' presenters.

You'll need a whole day to even attempt to take all this in and I can tell you now you'll be knackered by the end of it.

Food prices aren't bad considering how they could rip you off. And there's a nice place to eat on the top floor too.

Although it might be freezing and bleak outside in Birmingham in December, inside it's like Majorca in the high season, so takes lots of 'easy-to-strip-off' layers and wear comfy shoes. We walked literally miles! But it was worth every painful second.

Just like a concert, you can't experience the atmosphere unless you go there yourself.

'Clothes Show Live' runs for one week in December every year.

Details appear in 'Clothes Show Live' magazine and other national press publications.

[N.B. This was presented in columns by the student with suitable
Headings and sub-heads]

Candidate's Commentary

The purpose of my article is to inform my audience about 'Clothes Show Live'. It is intended for publication in a teenage/young adult's magazine such as *More* or *19* and may be read by either males or females. This is the reason for the entertainment aspect of the article, which is essential for publication in such a magazine, and the conversational tone I have adopted throughout.

The introductory paragraph is written in short, sharp, declarative sentences, which are all simple sentences. The verbs used are in the present tense. My intention here was to create a feeling of anticipation before an event [as yet unnamed] takes place. I also informed the audience of my own presence at the event by my use of the personal pronoun 'we'.

The description of the show itself is also in the present tense. Here I hoped to involve the audience by making them feel as if it were happening now. It is in this paragraph that words from the lexical set of 'fashion' appear. Although some people might not understand the references made, the audience for whom I am writing would be sure to.

I carefully chose the verb 'to prowl' to describe the models walking down the catwalk. As most people know, models must adopt a particular gait to move along the catwalk. It is intended to show off the clothes, together with the grace and beauty of the model's body. Thinking about this reminded me of a cat prowling, which is why the verb is used. It also creates a strong image, which is very important, as I would like the readers to visualise the show. Imagery does not only appear in the description of the catwalk, but in the whole piece. At one point during the article I have declared that, 'It may be freezing outside in December, but inside it's like Majorca in the high season.' This sentence uses simile to heighten the imagery but also introduces contrast. Contrasts are used in the writing to add light, shade and depth. The contrasts also use colloquial language which is relevant to the register which I have tried to make consistent through the whole piece.

I thought long and hard about how to introduce the next paragraph. This had to be full of information about the show itself. As I had just written about a glamorous scene I decided to continue the theme by asking the reader to think where we were. Paris, Milan and New York are the three most popular cities for designers to show off their clothes – Birmingham is not!

A series of questions is arresting. Questions can alter the pace of a piece of writing and therefore suggest a feeling. In my writing the questions are short and sharp and quicken the pace to indicate excitement. This is a common literary device, which fulfilled my intentions by introducing the surprise aspect of my being in Birmingham. The next paragraph contains more information about the show. It is written in declarative sentences, as most informative pieces would be. I have, in an attempt to maintain the correct register, introduced a little humour in the last line.

The next section begins with an imperative directly addressed to the audience. The description has an abundance of nouns and verbs, as I wanted to be very exact about what was happening in as few words as possible. It is also for this reason that all the information appears in one sentence which contains six clauses packed with information. The conversational tone continues in phrases such as 'Fancy yourself as the new Cindy, Christy or Linda?' This sentence contains both colloquial language and 'references for the initiated', ie the names of the models. These references appear elsewhere in the article and are usually concerned with the names of people famous in the world of fashion and design. The intended audience would definitely understand these references, which is why no explanation is given.

Although the writing moves through stages of both subjectivity and objectivity, it is never persuasive. Use of adjectives is usually extremely subjective. It is in this piece as they convey my own opinions. 'Magical scene' gives my impression but does not suggest that they should agree or disagree.

Certain small changes were made to the vocabulary between drafts. When describing the NEC, I changed 'enormity' to 'vastness' as I felt that the word 'enormity' is, today, generally associated with things going wrong. I also changed 'diversity' to 'variety' simply for the sake of style and to avoid repetition.

The word 'hairovers' which appears is interesting. I wrote it without thinking but noticed when rereading the piece. I could not find this in any dictionary. I therefore presume it is a neologism derived from 'hair' and the more common 'makeover' to produce a new coinage, which means 'to have a new hairstyle.'

'Surrender themselves to the scissors' is a phrase I used deliberately to keep my language informal and entertaining. It is interesting as the use of alliteration unifies the language and foregrounds the idea of being helpless in the hands of the stylist.

Another interesting linguistic feature I picked up at the show was the use of the word 'horny'. To the generation attending the show it means particularly good looking and not, as it might to an older reader, a reference to sexual excitement.

The conversational tone, which is meant to characterise the article, is particularly apparent in the lines, 'We must have walked literally miles! But it was worth every painful second.' People use the word 'literally' very carelessly in conversation (though in this case it is literal!). The second sentence starts with a conjunction – this too is a feature of informal conversation.

To conclude the article I made another reference to something else the audience would identify with – a pop concert. I decided to add a few details regarding dates and how to obtain tickets for 'Clothes Show Live' as this is a common feature of magazine articles such as the one I have written.

Moderator's report

Has it already been mentioned how important personal engagement with the material is? The point is being hammered deliberately. All the examples of student work used in this book have started from personal experience and have gained strength because of it!

This writer attended the 'Clothes Show Live' and his enthusiasm comes through in the article.

Having chosen to aim at a teenage readership the writer tailors his language to that audience. The commentary shows how register (the link between language and audience) has been carefully chosen and conscious efforts have been made to ensure that this is consistent throughout. The writer makes a number of references to colloquialisms and their importance. He also shows awareness of how conversation differs from formal, written English.

Other techniques of writing for this audience are also considered; pacing is explained, as is the element of humour. The writer also shows knowledge of grammar and how it works to enhance meaning. Professor David Crystal states that nouns, verbs, adjectives etc are the bricks that language is built with but that grammar is the mortar that holds them together and gives them meaning. The commentary demonstrates understanding of this principle.

The writer further shows how he has considered his audience with what he calls 'references for the initiated', which he uses at least three times.

Minor changes to vocabulary between drafts are noted as are features of magazine articles that provided the models for this one. (It is always a good idea to show how models have been used. In this case the student included samples from *More!* and *19* to show how he had attempted to follow a 'house style'.)

A number of linguistic devices are highlighted, for example, the use of alliteration, but notice that the writer states why he chose to use it; not merely that he has. He also covers his use of the present tense to suggest immediacy and importance of contrasts in the writing.

The student also followed a line of enquiry when he realised that he had used a word picked up at the show without considering it until he looked at his draft. His conclusion about the coinage of 'hairover' is almost certainly correct.

Though the primary purpose of this 'Clothes Show Live' is to inform, the writer acknowledges that it is possible to have a number of writing purposes in the same piece and there is a necessary, given the audience, element of entertainment in the article.

This candidate has a very clear idea of the purpose and process of writing. He explains his decisions regarding choice of words and is aware of the demands of writing for this audience.

Summary

First and foremost, the commentary should throw light on the process of writing:

- Why was the piece written?
- Who was it written for?
- How did the piece develop through drafts and revisions?
- If there have been deletions or additions or substitution of words or phrases, why was the change made and how did it improve the writing?
- If the piece were shown to an audience, did their response provoke any alterations or would you still defend your original choice of words?
- How did you decide on a format? If you have used a particular magazine or type of story, submit it with your commentary and explain how it influenced your own writing.
- If you have submitted a coursework folder which contains a number of different pieces it can be extremely useful to contrast the styles, registers and formats you have used.
- A reflection on your own developing skills as a writer over your course can be constructive.
- It is useful on occasion to write a 'pre-commentary' in which you set out what you are hoping to achieve and how you hope to achieve it. This can provide you with a starting point for your closing commentary. For example, 'When I set out to write this piece I intended to write a light-hearted article but my research made me change my approach.'

Final thoughts

Writing is like any exercise or skill, the more you do it, the better you will get at it. If you constantly evaluate your work and listen to people who might be able to help, you are bound to improve.

You probably wouldn't attempt to run the 1500 metres without some training – regard your drafts as training sessions that will help you to peak at the correct time.

6 Story Writing

In many ways, this is the most difficult type of assignment you can attempt as part of your A-Level course. This is because of the limitations of word counts for coursework and of time in examinations. If you're not careful, what you end up with is an anecdote rather than a genuine short story.

So what's the difference? Basically, an anecdote is merely a short account of an incident from one's own life or something that we've heard about.

A pupil at a school in Liverpool told the Head of Technology that demolition workers engaged nearby had offered some timber to the school. The offer had been gratefully received and the pupil said he and his friends would collect the timber and bring it to school. The timber turned out to be a coffin – the building being demolished was an undertaker's. The coffin was put in a storeroom while the technology department decided what to do with it. Meanwhile, the cleaning ladies refused to clean the woodwork room.

As this stands it's an anecdote. There is no attempt to define a location other than 'a school', there are no specific characters and nothing happens. The anecdote could be developed, however. Let's imagine that the boys who are bringing the coffin into school don't just carry it the few hundred metres from the demolition site but put one of their number into it with his eyes closed, arms folded across his chest and a flower on his chest, the flower being pinched from a graveyard, perhaps. They walk slowly to school with the now occupied coffin on their shoulders. Let's further imagine the reaction of others in the locality, which could range from disgust to incredulity. To say nothing of the bus driver who is so amazed by the procession that he almost loses control of his vehicle. Let's say that the Headteacher is understandably angry that local residents are telephoning the school to complain about the behaviour of the boys and tells the technology teacher to sort it out quickly. Perhaps his explanation that the school drama group is about to start rehearsing *Dracula* doesn't satisfy the cleaners and they refuse to go anywhere near his room till the coffin is removed. The next day the school is to admit a pupil who has been excluded from his previous school for attempted arson. By chance, the first lesson on his timetable is woodwork and he manages to be late despite the fact that the woodwork room is next door to his form room and his attitude is confrontational to say the least. The teacher shows him the coffin and tells him that it is kept there for pupils who offend against the school code of conduct as the Headteacher is a man of violent temper and coffins are needed on a regular basis. Collapse of aggressive pupil!

This is still not a story but it's more developed than the first, anecdotal, version in that there are characters who could be developed, a plot of sorts and opportunities to add details which would provide 'colour' to the narrative such as the astonished bus driver and the irate local people.

ACTIVITY 28

The following anecdotes have all been taken from one day's edition of a national newspaper and each has the potential to be developed into a short story. Choose one of these items and 'flesh it out' so that it now has the kind of detail as that of the second version of the 'coffin' story.

1 Fifty-four fruit pickers are being quizzed after a swoop by police to check on illegal immigrants.
You could consider how the immigrants got into the country, why they were engaged on this job, how the police became suspicious.

2 A deodorant company is advertising for four 'sensory assessors' to smell under the armpits of volunteers testing new products.
The job pays £10,000 per year. Who would want a job such as this? A teenage boy who thinks it might get him near girls? What would an interview for a job like this consist of?

3 Landscape gardeners unearthed a wartime grenade in a picnic area. It was defused by experts.
Where was the grenade? A busy park? Whose position would this be told from? A bomb disposal expert? A mother whose toddler discovered the grenade and thought it was a toy?

4 A teacher set a new world record by staying on a rollercoaster for 770 hours. He intends to stay on the rollercoaster until he's clocked 1000 hours.
Why would he do this? To impress his pupils who called him a wimp? His girlfriend who challenged him to get on the television news?

5 A football fan named his baby Michael Owen David Seaman after his two World Cup heroes.
Did his wife object? Perhaps she's a Scot! Was she still under the influence of painkillers and unaware what he'd done? Perhaps the father registered the child as Michael Owen David Seaman and his wife didn't find out till afterwards. She thought her son's name was Keanu Leonardo!

6 A Russian boy of six years old lived for two years with a pack of stray dogs who protected him from harm.
Scope for fantasy here – could the boy speak to the dogs just as Tarzan could communicate with jungle animals? How would he adapt to living among humans again?

These anecdotes are offered in answer to the inevitable question, 'Where do short stories come from?' If you want to write a short story but can't think of a topic you could do a lot worse than look in the newspapers.

It started with a theme

Another way to begin is to think of a theme. There are many books about writing, from writing short stories to writing blockbuster novels by way of writing romances and historical novels and each one will tell you that there are a limited number of themes. Unfortunately no two books can agree on what this number is. But that won't stop us suggesting some major themes for short stories to you!

Betrayal – this doesn't have to be on a national or international scale. In fact, for a short story it should be kept quite intimate, such as the revelation of a secret a character wanted kept hidden. In Shakespeare's *Othello*, Iago betrays the trust Othello has in him because of his jealousy.

The Quest – a character wants to succeed at something and sets out to accomplish his/her goal. Usually in the course of a 'quest' plot the central character learns something about him/herself and changes as a result. If you decide on this type of story ensure that you explain the point of the quest early on. Jason sets out in search of the Golden Fleece in the belief that this will help him regain his throne.

Thwarted Love – characters meet, fall in love but are kept apart through circumstances such as family objections. Does *Romeo & Juliet* ring a bell?

Requited Love – characters fall in love and, after a series of mishaps and misunderstandings which could have spoiled things, live happily ever after. The problem here is to avoid stereotypes as the central characters, unless, of course, you are using stereotypes deliberately to set up expectations you're going to shatter with a twist in the tail ending. Again think of Shakespeare and the plot of *Much Ado About Nothing*, or Charlotte Brontë's *Jane Eyre*.

The Cinderella Syndrome – a character who is looked down on eventually comes out on top because of their inherent goodness or some other quality. Remember here that your reader has got to sympathise with the underdog so do try to make him/her interesting to the reader rather than bland and colourless. Rita in Willy Russell's play *Educating Rita* overcomes the objections of her family to gain the education she missed out on at school.

The Innocent Abroad – the character who appears to be naïve and even hopeless who succeeds through sheer optimism. A modern example of this would be *Forrest Gump*.

Rivalry – a good choice for the short story writer. Read Hemingway's *The Old Man and the Sea* to see what can be done in relatively few pages. In this type of story your characters should be well-matched otherwise one of them is the underdog and you might end up with a Cinderella story.

Metamorphosis (a dramatic change) – such as occurs in Bram Stoker's *Dracula*, in which the Transylvanian count becomes a vampire bat by night, or the comic book *The Incredible Hulk*, based on Stevenson's *Dr Jekyll and Mr Hyde* in which the research scientist Bruce Banner, after exposure to gamma radiation saving the life of a teenager who has managed to get onto a nuclear testing station, becomes the super-powered Hulk in moments of stress.

Coming of age – these stories usually concern a character on the verge of adulthood who, through overcoming some fear or facing some challenge, begins to mature. Doris Lessing's *Through the Tunnel*, about a boy who tests his endurance by swimming underwater through a tunnel despite his fears, is an excellent example of such a story.

Of course, each of these themes can be treated in a number of ways either by being written in different genres: comedy, tragedy, soap-opera, adventure, thriller, science fiction or by being written for different audiences. For example, *Raiders of the Lost Ark* is a quest story treated as straightforward adventure. And the theme of rivalry runs through just about every television soap opera.

Choosing an anecdote or theme to develop is only the beginning. You have a number of other issues to consider:

The opening

How are you going to ensure your reader stays with you? Possible strategies include:

- intriguing the reader in some way – hinting at details of something to be revealed
- creating suspense in the opening paragraph – perhaps by opening with a tense, dramatic moment
- setting out a problem, quest, secret or mystery
- use of contrasts or shock tactics
- introducing a character(s) with whom the reader can empathise or feel antipathy to
- describing a scene so dramatically or realistically that the reader is immediately drawn into the location.

As an example of an opening which intrigues look at how Ray Bradbury opens *A Sound of Thunder*.

TEXT 35

The sign on the wall seemed to quaver under a film of sliding warm water. Eckels felt his eyelids blink over his stare, and the sign burned in this momentary darkness:

TIME SAFARI, INC.
SAFARIS TO ANY YEAR IN THE PAST.
YOU NAME THE ANIMAL.
WE TAKE YOU THERE.
YOU SHOOT IT.

Here we are faced immediately with the incredible idea of time travel but not time travel alone; time travel for the purposes of hunting and killing animals. We immediately wonder about the morality of such an idea and are drawn into the story.

The writer H. P. Lovecraft is generally regarded as a master of the Gothic horror story. Look at how he opens his short story *Dagon*. Dagon, Lovecraft explains, is the Fish-God referred to in Philistine legend.

TEXT 36

Dagon
I am writing this under an appreciable mental strain, since by tonight I shall be no more. Penniless, and at the end of my supply of the drug which alone makes life endurable, I can bear the torture no longer: and shall cast myself from this garret window into the squalid street below. Do not think from my slavery to morphine that I am a weakling or a degenerate. When you have read these hastily scrawled pages you may guess, though never fully realise, why it is that I must have forgetfulness or death.

There are many 'hooks' in this paragraph to attract the reader to continue. For example:

- why is the narrator so determined to end his life this particular night?
- what has he experienced that has left him dependent on morphine?
- what is it that can only be escaped by 'forgetfulness or death'?

Choose one of the themes listed earlier and write a number of possible openings to a short story based on that theme. Ask yourself should I concentrate:

- on setting an interesting scene?
- on introducing an intriguing character?

- on dropping hints about what is to follow in the story?
- on using familiar references so the reader feels comfortable?

This, after all, is what Bradbury and Lovecraft have done.

Plot construction

So, you have an opening which is arresting and interesting. Where do you go from here?

You may find the 5W+H formula useful, especially if you're faced with the task of producing a short story in an examination time and won't have time for numerous drafts. Of course, the formula can still be useful if you have got time. The 5W+H formula stands for:

Who? – What? – Why? – When? – Where? – How?

Who? – these are the characters in your story. In a short story it's wise not to have too many major characters but know them! You might have taken part in a drama exercise called 'hot-seating' during which a student is asked questions about the character they are playing to test that they understand that character. Mentally 'hot-seat' your character. What is his/her name? How old is he/she? What kind of person is he/she? You may not use all the details of character and background you create in your story but your handling of their character should be consistent. It's not enough to state 'Jane was a helpful kind of girl' unless you put Jane in a situation which will allow her to demonstrate this aspect of her character. In a short story you have to show as well as tell. It's also a good idea in a short story to establish early on who the main protagonist is and from whose point of view the story is being told.

What? – this refers to the event which is the catalyst for the story. It's usually an event, though it could be a person. This event could be in the form of a challenge. In Frederick Forsyth's *The Dogs of War*, a mercenary, Cat Shannon, has to put together a small force of soldiers and plan the storming of a presidential palace. Much of the novel is to do with how he prepares for the action.

Why? – this arises out of the who? and what? sections. Why is the character so interested/involved in the action of the story? It's to do with your character's motivation. Why does Yossarian in Joseph Heller's *Catch 22* behave so outrageously? The answer is that he wants to survive the war and will do anything, no matter how insane it appears, to accomplish this.

When? – if your story is taking place in 'the now' you probably won't have to go into any detail which fixes it in a particular period. If it happens to be Tuesday you just have a character say 'I hate Tuesdays!' but if your story is set in the past or the future you may have to go into more detail. This can be done by baldly stating: 'It was December in the year 1066 and William the Conqueror had just been crowned King of England.' You could refer to events or characters which would enable your reader to build a picture gradually about the time in which your story is set.

Where? – place names only go a little way to creating a sense of location, though if your story were to be set in Camelot most of your readers would have a good idea of what to expect. Similarly, fans of *Conan the Barbarian* would know what to expect if a story was set in Hyperborea. You can, as omnipotent narrator, tell your readers about the location for the story or you can allow details to come out through the comments of your characters.

How? – this refers to how your character carries out the 'why' of the story. In a well-planned story there will be obstacles to how the action is carried out which will add interest to the plot and allow you to reveal your protagonist's strengths and weaknesses. In the Frederick Forsyth novel referred to above, the plan is complicated by the presence of a rival mercenary who wanted the same assignment, by a well-meaning academic unsure of the morality of the situation and by many other twists in the plot.

So far in this section we have looked at story writing in very general terms so let's be more specific and examine a type of short story which is very popular with A-Level candidates – the short story published in 'Women's Magazines' – though not all the readers of these magazines are female. Don't make the mistake, as some candidates do, of writing a story and stating baldly, 'My story is for a woman's magazine', and go on to demonstrate that they have probably never read one or if they have, they have read with little understanding of the genre.

A look at four 'women's magazines' in one week shows that all run short stories under series titles which indicate that the stories are not too long or challenging.

Magazine	Series Title
Take A Break	Coffee Break
Best	Best short story collection
Woman's Own	Take Five
Chat	5 minute fiction

More detailed examination shows that the shortest of the stories was 930 words in length while the longest was 1007 words long. The average number of paragraphs in the four stories was 34. Three out of the four were written in the third person while one was in the first. Three stories used the simple past tense while one used the present. Dialogue accounted for between 23% and 50% of the texts.

This is the kind of preparation you need to undertake if you're going to write a story in this genre. It is no use writing a story over 2000 words in length, with a complicated list of characters and convoluted plot if you are then going to state that you wrote it for a publication such as one of the above.

ACTIVITY 30

Story writing assignment

The D. C. Thomson magazine *The People's Friend* was founded in 1869 and carries on average six short stories each week which vary in length between 1,000 and 4,000 words. The editors state that they want stories about ordinary characters with the kind of problems that the average reader can identify with. They look for romantic and emotional developments in the characters rather than complicated or contrived plots.

The magazine is aimed at an older audience. This means that language used tends to be 'gentle'. Characters do not use profanities or obscenities.

Read the extract from 'First Impressions' and complete the story in your own way. Before you start you should look at features such as sentence and paragraph length, use of dialogue and vocabulary level. When you have done this, read the author's own version which is given at the end of this chapter.

TEXT 37

First Impressions

Arthur didn't know that his adored new wife had already met his darling daughter . . . and that it had been a complete disaster!

HELEN BAINES watched from the gate as Arthur's car edged out of the close into the morning traffic. Her face was relaxed, her brown eyes shining after his parting kiss. After six months of marriage – the second for both of them – they were still behaving like a couple of young lovers, grudging every moment they had to spend apart.

She turned and walked slowly back to the bungalow, pausing to nip off the broken head of an overblown dahlia. The tall clumps of Michaelmas daisies and chrysanthemums were weighted with the first mists of autumn, and there was a decided nip in the air.

She shivered, her mood changing. When Arthur got back from the airport, his daughter Lucy would be with him.

Helen's little deception would be out in the open, and, unless Lucy had changed, their happiness might well be threatened.

Last night she had tried again to tell him.

"About Lucy, dear . . . why she didn't come to our wedding . . . I think I may know . . ."

"She couldn't get away – pressure of work. She told us!"

He'd pulled her closer to him and kissed her hair.

"Now, stop worrying. You'll love her, and she'll soon realise she has the best stepmother a girl could wish for!"

Weakly, she'd buried her face in his shoulder. It was so much safer than telling him that she and Lucy had met before, and it hadn't exactly been a happy experience . . .

Before you start, let's consider what clues can be picked up from the opening section.

We learn that:

- Helen and Arthur have been married six months and that it is the second marriage for both of them.
- Arthur has a daughter, Lucy, from his previous marriage who did not attend his wedding to Helen.
- Helen thinks she knows the reason why Lucy didn't attend.
- Helen has a secret – she has already met Lucy (remember Nick Warburton's advice on giving characters a secret in the radio writing section on page 18).

Notice how the synopsis under the title tells us most of this. This sentence:

Arthur didn't know his new wife had already met his darling daughter … and that it had been a complete disaster!

acts as a hook to draw the reader into the story in the same way that the 'blurb' on the back of a novel does. A few important details of the plot are revealed, but not enough to give away the whole story.

Remember the editor's instructions:

- the story should have 'ordinary' characters
- problems the readers can identify with
- romantic developments
- simple plots
- write for an audience that tends to be older.

The writer is warned off complex plots but there a number of questions arising from this opening section.

Does the story need more characters? If you decide 'Yes' remember that too many will clutter up the plot and you might have difficulties making them interesting or relevant.

Given that the stories should be romantic, that Helen is described as an 'adored new wife' and Lucy as Arthur's 'darling daughter', is it likely that any tragedy or melodrama will be found in the story? So what might have occurred that 'hadn't exactly been a happy experience …' and why hadn't Helen told Arthur about meeting Lucy?

As the meeting obviously took place before the wedding you should consider:

- how Helen and Arthur met
- why they are on their second marriages
- where has Lucy been? As Arthur is going to meet her at the airport she's probably been abroad. Who with? And for how long?

Look at the language of the opening section. Would you say that the vocabulary was difficult? Are the paragraphs long? The answer to both these questions is obviously 'No'. Keep this in mind when constructing your own story.

Alternatively, you could choose a publication or genre you are more familiar with and, after going through the same preliminaries, attempt to write a story for that magazine.

Writing for children

This is, in some ways, a more difficult and challenging task than writing for an adult audience. If you write for a general adult audience your story will generally be acceptable to a wide range of readers. However, a 7 year old could not, in every case, understand a story written for a 10 year old and children who have to be read to will not want the kind of story that a child who can read for him/herself would enjoy. This means that as an author you are restricted in terms of the vocabulary you can use or the kind of theme you choose for your children's story.

When writing for a young readership there are four principles which should always guide you.

1 Never write down to your audience.
2 Always be sure of your facts, even when writing fiction.
3 Children who are reading for themselves often like to read about characters slightly older than themselves while children who are read to often prefer characters of their own age.
4 Young readers/listeners also need to be given security in their reading. They prefer to have a solid, identifiable location and the presence of reliable, older people on whom they can rely.

The student who produced *Boris the Spider* chose to have a spider rather than a human as his central character but gave Boris a number of human characteristics which would be shared with the target audience. The writer also analysed his own vocabulary to check that his audience would be able to cope by themselves but acknowledged that children tend to 'read above their age' and need some vocabulary to stretch their abilities.

TEXT 38

There once was a spider.

His name was Boris.

Boris liked spinning webs,

and climbing.

One day Boris got tired of spinning webs.

He was bored -

Then he had an idea!

"I think I will build a rocket." Thought Boris.
So Boris set about finding all the things he would need to build his rocket.

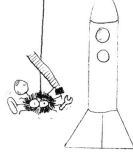

He put them all together and soon his rocket was finished.

ACTIVITY 31

Write your own story for a young audience. As always, you should do some preliminary reading to see what length, number of words per page and subject matter are favoured by your target audience. If you are intending to submit a story for this age group as part of a coursework submission you will find it extremely useful if you can trial your story.

The reaction of your audience will help you no end with redrafting and writing a commentary.

TEXT 31

Below is a list of 200 of the most common words a child should know.

200 COMMON WORDS A CHILD SHOULD KNOW

Twelve words make up on average one quarter of all reading.
These are as follows:

a	and	he	I	in	is	it	of	that
the	to	was						

The following twenty words together with the above twelve words (thirty-two words) make up on average one third of all reading.

all	as	at	be	but	are	for	had	have
him	his	not	on	one	said	so	they	we
with	you							

The following sixty-eight words together with the above thirty-two words (one hundred words) make up on average one half of all reading.

about	an	back	been	before	big	by	call	came
can	come	could	did	do	down	first	from	get
go	has	her	here	if	into	just	like	little
look	made	make	more	me	much	must	my	no
new	now	off	old	only	or	our	other	out
over	right	see	she	some	their	them	then	there
this	two	up	want	well	went	were	what	when
where	which	who	will	your				

The one hundred next most used words. Nouns in italics.

after	again	always	am	another	any	ask	away	bad
because	best	*bird*	black	blue	*boy*	bring	*day*	*dog*
don't	eat	every	far	fast	*father*	fell	find	*five*
fly	*four*	found	gave	*girl*	give	going	good	*got*
green	*hand*	*head*	help	*home*	*house*	how	jump	keep
know	last	left	let	live	long	*man*	many	may
men	*mother*	Mr	never	next	once	open	own	play
put	ran	read	red	*room*	round	run	sat	saw
say	*school*	should	sing	*sit*	soon	stop	take	tell
then	these	*thing*	think	*three*	*time*	too	*tree*	under
us	very	walk	white	why	wish	work	would	*year*
yes								

As you can see from the table, over half of all reading can be done with this basic vocabulary. When you have completed your own story check the vocabulary against the list of 200 words. Is your vocabulary choice suitable or have you used too many words which might be unfamiliar to the audience and so put them off?

What do we need to consider, then, when story writing?

- The audience – what are their needs and expectations?
- The beginning – does it grip the reader? Does it establish mood, location, theme or character?
- What is the time scheme for the story? You are unlikely to be able to fit a convincing space epic or dynastic saga within the word count you have to adhere to.
- What genre are you writing in? Is it a thriller, science-fiction, romance, children's story, comedy? This is, of course, tied to your chosen theme – something we looked at at the start of this section.
- How many locations and characters are going to be used?
- Can you plot your story marking any climaxes, twists or surprises?
- What issues do you want to raise in the minds of your readers?
- Have you got a satisfying ending?
- Have you studied your market?

Happy writing!

First Impressions (Text 37) – original ending

After Gordon's death, she'd gone back to work in a city office. If they'd had a family she would have felt less lonely. But if there had been children, she would have had less time and strength to devote to Gordon in his last years.

"Keep yourself busy," everyone had advised, and it had seemed sensible.

She had battled on for two years, learning the new hi-tech office skills and commuting almost two hours every day, until it all seemed utterly pointless.

She had already decided to look for a job nearer home when she saw Arthur's advertisement in the local paper.

Mature lady required to keep house for businessman. Hours to suit.

Arthur Baines was a few years older than herself. He was quietly spoken and courteous – the sort of man she would be happy to work for.

"My daughter is away at university most of the time," he'd told her. "But there would be two

of us to look after now and again."

That didn't worry Helen. She'd agreed to go every weekday.

It was a lovely old house, though neglected, and she'd enjoyed getting it back into shape. It was satisfying, too, to be preparing proper meals again.

There hadn't been any reason to do so after Gordon died. She began to cook for herself at home, too. Life seemed much less bleak.

The first time Lucy was due home, Gordon's sister had to go

into hospital and needed help with the children. Arthur had been most understanding. Helen had prepared meals in advance and left a well-stocked freezer.

On her next holiday, Lucy had spent only a couple of weekends at home.

"She spends a lot of time with her boyfriend's family, down on the coast," Arthur told her. "Rob's a great chap . . . training to be a doctor. It must be dull for her around here."

She hadn't realised Arthur was divorced until the long summer break came round.

"Lucy will be dropping in for a change of clothes," he'd said with a wry smile, "before she jets off to New York to stay with her mother and stepfather."

He lives for that girl, Helen thought, and he gets so little of her company.

She planned her future time off to coincide with Lucy's visits. That way, her father could enjoy every minute with her without a third party in the way.

She handed him a list of menus she had made out, and instructions which meals to use first.

"You spoil me, Helen." He shook his head, smiling. "You think of everything!"

They discovered a shared taste in music one day when Arthur came home to find her mending shirts to the sound of a radio concert. He encouraged her to borrow from his large collection of tapes, and this made another talking-point when they had a weekly cup of tea together on Friday afternoons.

He had taken to coming home early before she finished for the week and, as time went by, he confided in her.

As Lucy's final exams approached, he was anxious, yet pleased.

"Whatever the results, she'll be home for a while. At least, until she finds a job, or . . ." he mused, hopefully ". . . she and Rob might get

married. I know she cares for him very much."

WHEN the end of term came and Lucy was expected home on the Saturday evening, her father made no secret of his pleasure.

Helen made and iced a cake at home and took it round early on the Saturday morning as her contribution to the welcome. It was raining heavily by the time she reached the back door which led into a utility room off the kitchen.

She was peeling off her wet things when she heard voices coming from upstairs. One, a female, and strident.

She had just taken off her shoes when a young woman charged through the kitchen carrying a suitcase in one hand, a bulging holdall in the other. She stopped suddenly when she saw Helen, who looked up and smiled.

"Oh, hello! You must be Lucy."

"And you must be the perfect Helen, I suppose!"

She gave Helen a long, venomous stare then pushed rudely past her, out of the door. An engine started up then there was a crunch of gravel as she drove off, presumably in the car which had been parked outside the garage.

Helen felt sick and dazed. The ugly little incident had hurt more than a physical blow.

How could such a dear, good man have such an unpleasant child? Instinctively, she wanted to rush in and console him.

Then, the second shock hit her. It was unthinkable – disloyal to dear Gordon.

She shook her head impatiently. But the fact remained – she was in love with Arthur.

He came into the kitchen looking drawn and pale.

"Helen! I didn't expect you today."

She fumbled into her outdoor shoes again, reluctant to meet his eyes. She was already on the verge of tears. She couldn't mention Lucy's name, let alone her behaviour.

"I thought I might have left my reading glasses behind yesterday," she improvised.

"I see." He nodded. "Lucy came home last night. She's gone to stay with a girl friend for a day or two." His voice trailed off and he looked at her, hesitated, then cleared his throat.

"Now that the rain is letting up," he went on hurriedly, "I think I'll play a round of golf this morning. You will be here on Monday?"

She tried to avoid him the following week, but on Friday he came home even earlier than usual.

"Helen, I think it's time the tables were turned," he announced decisively.

"I'm sorry . . . ?"

"It's time I gave you a meal, for a change. Would you let me take you out to lunch one day?"

Seeing her hesitation, he added, "Just to say thank you?"

They had gone to a pleasant country pub and talked companionably about their common interests; music, books, gardening and – eventually – about Lucy.

"She's decided to make her home in the States," he told her. "Her stepfather has taken her into his advertising agency. It's a great opportunity.

"My only regret is that she has broken with Rob. I thought he was just right for her, too. Ah, well . . ." He smiled across at her. "We all make mistakes."

The next time he asked her out, she hesitated only briefly. They went to the same place and he told her about his marriage.

"Celia is lovely – and talented – but she soon discovered she wasn't a home-maker. She resented every day she had to be away from work. When Lucy was old enough, she took a job in advertising and made a great success of it.

"She moved in another world, really. I couldn't keep up with her. Then she met another high-flyer – an American – and we gave up pretending.

"I did persuade her to stay until

Lucy was old enough to cope with it. There had never been any question of her going to New York with her mother. She was so happy at her school and that suited Celia."

"It must have been a very difficult time for you."

"It was." He smiled wryly. "But that's enough about the past." he lowered his voice.

"You know, the food here isn't a patch on yours!"

The Sunday outings gradually became a habit . . . a good one, Helen felt. She no longer felt disloyal. She had been there for Gordon when he needed her, and part of her would always be his. But now, Arthur needed her as much as she needed him.

At the end of the year, he was asked to take early retirement. Shortly after, he asked her to marry him.

"I know it can only be second-best for you, Helen. I'm being utterly selfish . . ."

"You couldn't be selfish if you tried," Helen interrupted him, stretching out her hands to his. The gesture gave him his answer.

They found a pleasant bungalow near the sea, and had a quiet, spring wedding. Lucy sent an expensive present and a polite little note to say that she couldn't get away. Her father accepted it at face value, but Helen had her doubts.

Lucy had been in the States for just over a year, her only contact an occasional card to her father. When she phoned to say she was coming over and would like to stay for a night or two, Arthur was delighted.

He covered the mouthpiece with his hand and turned to Helen.

"We can put Lucy up for a couple of nights, can't we?"

"Of course, love. That will be nice."

But her qualms returned. It was ridiculous to feel guilty about that episode for which Lucy had been solely responsible. But whatever she said now in explanation of their meeting would rake up old hurts and might damage his trust in her.

THE lunch, at least, would be special. She'd prepared Lucy's favourite dishes, and laid the table with the elegant Fifth Avenue table-cloth and napkins which had been her wedding gift.

When Helen heard the car driving in, her heart lurched. She put on a smile and went to the door with an open mind.

Lucy seemed older, slimmer . . . slightly strained.

She came forward with her hand outstretched, head tilted to one side, a gesture borrowed from her father.

"Helen . . .?"

"Lucy! You're very welcome!"

They shook hands cautiously, unsure of what was to follow.

A tall, fair-haired young man had climbed out of the car, and Arthur was shepherding him towards the house.

"Ah, I see you two have met, at last! And this is Rob – Doctor Robert Bevans, I should say. An old friend . . . He and Lucy travelled over together. I've persuaded him to join us for lunch."

"I hope I'm not being a nuisance?" Rob smiled down at her as they shook hands.

He was as attractive and likeable as Arthur had described him. It seemed he had been on a course at a New York hospital, and had been in touch with Lucy for some time.

Helen was glad of his presence to distract attention from herself.

The meal was pleasant in every way. After they'd had coffee in the sitting-room, Rob looked at the clock, and then at Lucy.

"Well, I must make tracks for my parents' home. Thanks for a wonderful lunch, Mrs Baines . . . er, Helen."

"Must you go?" Lucy asked, frowning.

"Yes." Rob nodded. "But I'll be over tomorrow, as agreed." He kissed her tenderly.

Arthur offered to drive him the half-hour journey to his home, but Rob wouldn't hear of it.

"A lift to the station would be fine. You three will have a lot to talk about."

Helen assumed Lucy would go with him but instead, she followed into the kitchen.

"Can we have a word before Dad gets back?" she asked, sitting on one of the stools.

Helen dried her hands and joined her.

"Helen, I am so sorry about the first time we met."

"That's all right, Lucy. I expect it was a trying time for you . . . breaking up with Rob, I mean."

"That was only part of it. I did want to work in America – just for a while – but I hated leaving Rob – and Dad. One word from either of them and I'd probably have given up the idea."

She gave Helen a disarming smile.

"Rob didn't much like it, but he said I must start thinking for myself, making my own decisions. But Dad told me not even to think about him. 'I have Helen' is all he said. 'I haven't a care in the world!

"I admit I was very jealous – and angry. It seemed as if he didn't care whether I stayed or went."

Helen bit her lip, her eyes full of sympathy.

"He loves you so much. I'm sure he was just anxious for you to be happy."

"I know that, now. Mum told me the full story of their break-up, but I'm sorry I took it all out on you. You didn't tell Dad, did you?

"And you mustn't, either." Helen shook her head, and reached for Lucy's hand.

"Thanks. I can see why he looks so happy!"

She jumped up at the sound of the returning car.

"Stick by me again, Helen – please. Dad's about to get rather a shock. You, too!"

WHILE Lucy went to meet her father in the hall, Helen filled the kettle. As she set out the cups, she heard Arthur's voice.

"That's water under the bridge, darling . . . but thank you for saying it."

They came into the kitchen, smiling.

Lucy took a deep breath.

"Rob and I were married last week," she announced without warning. "We eloped! He starts work in London next month. We're going to spend our honeymoon flat-hunting!"

"Lucy!" Her father's surprise was swiftly followed by a hug. "Why didn't you tell us when Rob was here? You must have known how delighted I'd be!"

"Rob insisted I sort out one or two little matters first." She gave Helen the briefest of winks.

Helen added her congratulations and Arthur was about to ask another question, but Lucy spoke first.

"We decided we'd wasted enough time already and we wanted to avoid all the upheaval, so . . . we just did it!"

"What did your mother say?" Arthur asked.

"She was shattered to begin with, but she could see it was right for us.

She and Glen gave us a super impromptu party!"

Helen put a hand on Arthur's arm and looked into his shining eyes.

"Let's do the same, darling. Lucy must phone Rob to make plans . . ."

As Arthur put his arm around her shoulders, Helen was already planning a celebration cake, and this one would be eaten in joy.

The End